INSIDE IMPROVISATION

VOL. 1 «MELODIC STRUCTURES»

JERRY BERGONZI

© 1992/2019 by advance music GmbH, Mainz

All Rights Reserved.

No parts of this publication may be reproduced
stored in retrieval system, or transmitted, in any form or by any means,
electronic, mechanical, photocopying, recording, or otherwise
without prior written permission of Advance Music.

International Copyright Secured.

Edited by Jeri Di Marco

Musical Notation: Hans Gruber

Cover Design: Traugott Bratic

Production: Hans Gruber

Published by Advance Music.

ADV 14220

CONTENTS

INTRODUCTION 5

Section 1

I	Four Note Groupings 1 - 5 7
	Assignment I 20
	Tune #1 "Lady Duck" 20
	Tune #2 "On The Brink" 22
II	Mixing Up Permutations 25
	Assignment II 27
	Tune #3 "Lunar" 27
	Tune #4 "How Low The Sun" 28
III	Visualization 31
	Assignment III 34
	Tune #5 "Inside The Milky Way" 34
IV	The Creative Imagination 37
	Assignment IV 38
V	Editing 39
	Assignment V 42
VI	Key Centers 43
	Assignment VI 45
	Tune #6 "Brontosaurus Walk" 45
VII	Inversions 47
	Assignment VII 48
VIII	Practice Exercise 49

REVIEW SKILLS 51

Tune #7 "Lovers Again" 52
Tune #8 "You're The One" 55

Section 2

IX	Four Note Groupings 5 - 9 58
	Assignment IX 63
X	Avoid Notes 64
	Assignment X 65
	Tune #9 "Fangs From Afar" 66
XI	Upper Structure Groupings 9 - 13 69
	Assignment XI 73
XII	Additional Groupings 74
	Assignment XII 79
XIII	Mixing Groupings 80
	Assignment XIII 88

CONCLUSION 89

APPENDIX

Scale and Chord Charts 90
Audio Track List 96

INTRODUCTION

Inside Improvisation - Melodic Structures, is the first in a series of books which describe a simple and pragmatic approach to improvisation. While focussing on the jazz idiom, the techniques discussed are applicable to many styles of music and all instruments, be it rock guitar, jazz saxophone, or the solos of the fusion keyboardist. The system presented in this volume offers a tangible pathway to **inside** the creative imagination by getting **inside** harmony, **inside** the changes.

Improvisation is individual expression and only you can play you the best. This particular approach to that creative world is both concise and direct. It is easily accessible to the amateur musician yet it allows for the expanded studies of the more advanced player. While it is one of many systems which can be used to study improvisation, this is a proven method and has been used by many students and professionals.

In this first book the lessons focus on a numerical system which provide the student with an intervallic method for playing on chord changes while examining the similarities and relationships between different chords. It is a system which categorizes various melodic scale segments and describes step by step how to use these melodies in developing your solos. This book is designed so that you as a student have specific assignments to complete at the end of each chapter.

Using The Play Along Recording:

The accompanying recordings have been designed for use in conjunction with each of the chapter assignments. There are nine tunes, each played at a slow and then medium tempo. Piano players can eliminate the piano track by turning the right channel of your amplifier to "0", bass players can turn off the left channel. It is suggested that you practice each assignment with the recording first using the slower tempo and then moving on to the faster tempo once you have gained familiarity with the lesson.

For beginning players, scale and chord charts can be found in the Appendix.

On our website **www.schott-music.com/online-material** all audio files can be downloaded for free with the following voucher code: **M89SE3ZN**
Auf **www.schott-music.com/online-material** können alle Audio-Dateien mit dem folgenden Gutscheincode kostenlos heruntergeladen werden: **M89SE3ZN**

I FOUR NOTE GROUPINGS 1-5

The first order of business is to find melodies to play on chord changes that "fit" or sound "good" on changes. Of course, musical improvisation is a subjective art form and what sounds "right" or "good" to a player is entirely individual. Without wishing to impose style, the system described herein should be considered a means to an end!

The improvisor must first look to the chord scales which underlie the harmonic structure. Every chord has its own chord scale. If you know your major chord scales you will be able to use this system, if you do not, refer to the chord charts and scale charts in the back of the book. Assigning a number to each degree of the scale commonly facilitates chord and scale spellings.

"C" major scale with appropriate numerical designations.

Minor and dominant chord scales are both derived from the major scale. An explanation on how to determine these scales follows on page 9.

NUMBERING SCALE TONES

Note that whatever the scale, the first degree is assigned the number 1, the second, the number 2, and so on. When using the number system presented here, the root of the chord is always "1".

Also, the numbers refer to each note as they appear (with or without an accidental) in their appropriate scales. For example, a G dominant 7 chord has a natural F in its chord scale while a G major 7 chord has an F sharp in its scale. The number 7 refers to either F natural or F sharp depending on the chord being played. Similarly, when we refer to the 3 or the 7 of a minor chord, it means flat 3 or flat 7 since that is implicit in a minor scale.

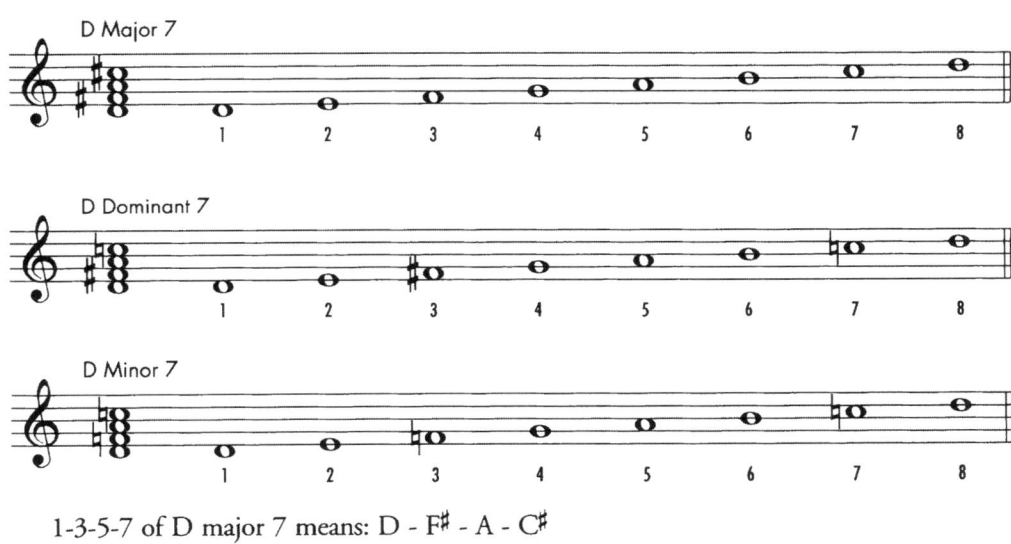

1-3-5-7 of D major 7 means: D - F♯ - A - C♯
1-3-5-7 of D dominant 7 means: D - F♯ - A - C
1-3-5-7 of D minor 7 means: D - F - A - C

FOUR NOTE GROUPINGS: 1-2-3-5, 1-3-4-5

Because there are unlimited possibilities for playing melodies on any given chord, to make progress learning how to improvise it is necessary to limit the infinite musical options. Rather than using all of the notes in the chord scale, in the beginning we will concern ourselves with only four notes as it provides us a kind of jumping off point.

The four note melodic scale segment includes 1 - 2 - 3 - 5 of the major and dominant scales and 1 - 3 - 4 - 5 of the minor scales.

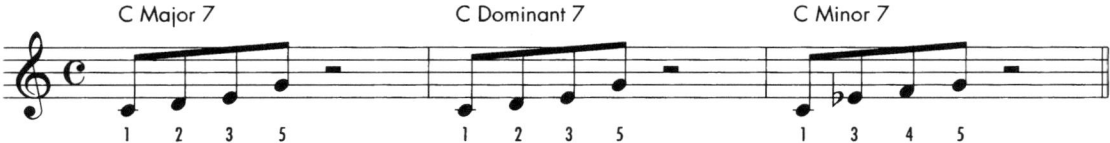

A grouping of four notes creates what is called a tetrachord and this particular grouping is one of the most natural sounding melodies that can be played on a chord.

WHY THESE NUMBERS? A THEORETICAL EXPLANATION

These 1 through 5 groupings of notes are derived from a series of fifths. Starting with C, build upwards in fifths; that is, C up a fifth to G, up a fifth to D, up a fifth to A, up a fifth to E. Arrange these notes in one octave and we have C-D-E-G-A which spells a major pentatonic scale. Rearranging the notes by putting "A" on the bottom creates a minor pentatonic scale. This series of notes forms two different four note groupings; starting on C, 1-2-3-5, and putting A on the bottom, 1-3-4-5.

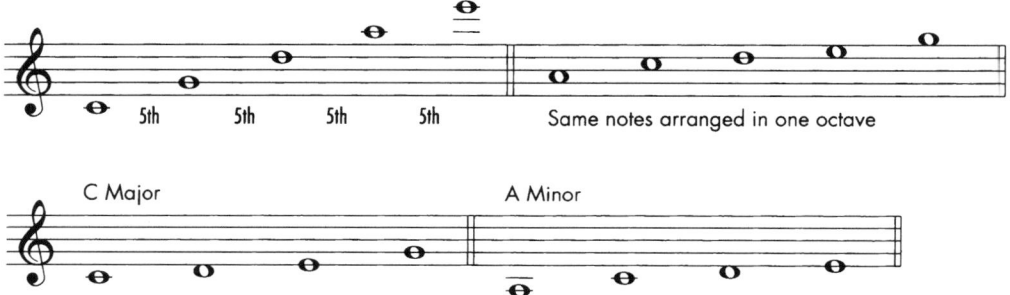

A relationship between the C major and A minor scales is then apparent. (Relative minor scales are a minor third below the major scale.) But the more important point being made here is that it is from this series of fifths that the numbers 1-2-3-5 for major and dominant chords and 1-3-4-5 for minor chords have been derived. This pyramid of fifths provides very consonant melodies that perfectly describe the sound of each chord.

Both sets of numbers, 1-2-3-5 for major and 1-3-4-5 for minor, contain the same intervals, that is, one minor third and two major seconds, thus keeping the melodies consistent with each other. Also, the notes A-C-D-E-G form what is called a mirror chord. From the center note of the chord, which is D, each half looks the same as the other. The intervals between the notes D, C, and A are the same as the ones between D, E, and G.

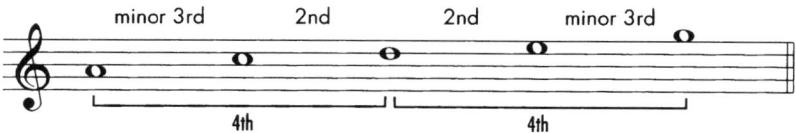

Not all are theory buffs so it doesn't matter if you understand the theory behind why these numbers were chosen. When you play them the sound will speak for itself!

THREE WAYS TO DETERMINE MINOR CHORD SCALES:

1. To determine a minor chord scale, take the major scale beginning with the same root and flat the third and seventh degrees.

    Example: To find a D minor chord scale; take the D major chord scale and lower the third and seventh by a half step. F sharp becomes F natural and C sharp becomes C natural in the minor scale.

2. You can spell a minor scale by using this formula:

    Root - whole step - half step - whole step - whole step - whole step - half step - whole step.

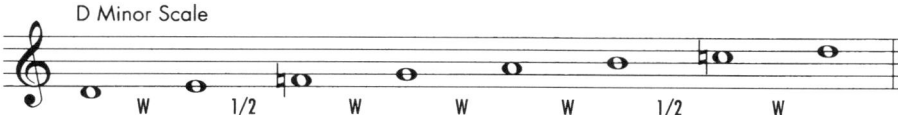

3. Make the root of the minor chord the second note of a major scale; then spell that major scale starting and ending on the root of the minor chord.

    Example: To find the appropriate scale for a D minor 7 chord, first answer the question: "D is the second note of what major scale?" "D" is the second note of a C major scale so spell the C major scale starting and ending on "D". The D minor scale looks the same as a C major scale (that is, no sharps or flats) but it starts and ends on "D".

THREE WAYS TO DETERMINE DOMINANT CHORD SCALES:

1. To determine a dominant chord scale, take the major scale beginning with the same root and flat the seventh degree.

    Example: To determine a G dominant 7 chord scale; take the G major chord scale and lower the seventh by a half step. F sharp becomes F natural in the dominant scale.

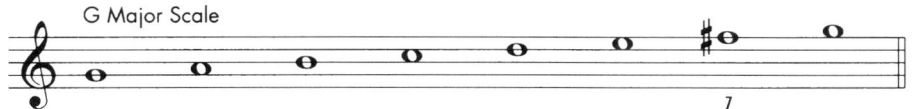

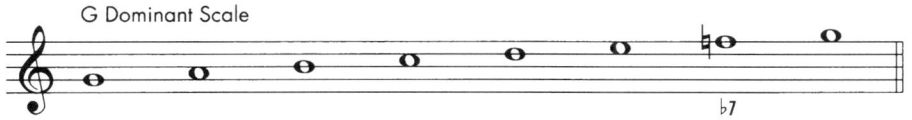

2. You can spell a dominant chord scale by using this formula:

Root - whole step - whole step - half step - whole step - whole step - half step - whole step.

3. Make the root of the dominant chord the fifth note of a major scale and spell that major scale starting and ending on the root of the dominant chord.

Example: To determine what chord scale is played over a G dominant 7 chord, first answer the question; "G is the fifth note of what major scale?". "G" is the fifth note of a C major scale, so again, spell the C major scale starting and ending "G".

PERMUTATIONS OF 1-5

The purpose of this four note system is to simplify and organize melodic material. Limiting the possibilities as you practice helps you to become familiar with the vast musical language available when improvising. Again, for this reason we are only concerning ourselves with four notes in the beginning and those four notes are 1-2-3-5 for major and dominant chords and 1-3-4-5 for minor chords.

1	2	3	5	Major and Dominant
1	3	4	5	Minor

The numbers 1-2-3-5 and 1-3-4-5 can then be arranged in 24 ways and these different arrangements of the four note melody are called permutations.

24 Permutations of 1-2-3-5

1 2 3 5	2 1 5 3	3 1 2 5	5 1 2 3
1 2 5 3	2 1 3 5	3 1 5 2	5 1 3 2
1 3 2 5	2 3 1 5	3 2 1 5	5 2 1 3
1 3 5 2	2 3 5 1	3 2 5 1	5 2 3 1
1 5 2 3	2 5 1 3	3 5 1 2	5 3 1 2
1 5 3 2	2 5 3 1	3 5 2 1	5 3 2 1

FOUR NOTE GROUPINGS 1-5

24 Permutations of 1-3-4-5

1 3 4 5	3 1 5 4	4 1 3 5	5 1 3 4
1 3 5 4	3 1 4 5	4 1 5 3	5 1 4 3
1 4 3 5	3 4 1 5	4 3 1 5	5 3 1 4
1 4 5 3	3 4 5 1	4 3 5 1	5 3 4 1
1 5 3 4	3 5 1 4	4 5 1 3	5 4 1 3
1 5 4 3	3 5 4 1	4 5 3 1	5 4 3 1

1-2-3-5 Permutations of a C Major chord

Note that because the difference between C major 7 and C dominant 7 is the seventh degree, the 1-2-3-5 sequence applies to both chords, that is, the seventh is not included in this grouping of notes.

I FOUR NOTE GROUPINGS 1-5

1-3-4-5 Permutations of a C Minor chord

1 3 4 5	3 1 5 4	4 1 5 3	5 1 3 4
1 3 5 4	3 1 4 5	4 1 3 5	5 1 4 3
1 4 3 5	3 4 1 5	4 3 1 5	5 3 1 4
1 4 5 3	3 4 5 1	4 3 5 1	5 3 4 1
1 5 3 4	3 5 1 4	4 5 1 3	5 4 1 3
1 5 4 3	3 5 4 1	4 5 3 1	5 4 3 1

If a chord has an alteration such as flat 9 or flat 5, make the appropriate alteration in your permutation. Nine is the same as two; see Chapter 10 for further explanation. Remember that the number 3 of a minor chord refers to the flat 3 of the minor scale.

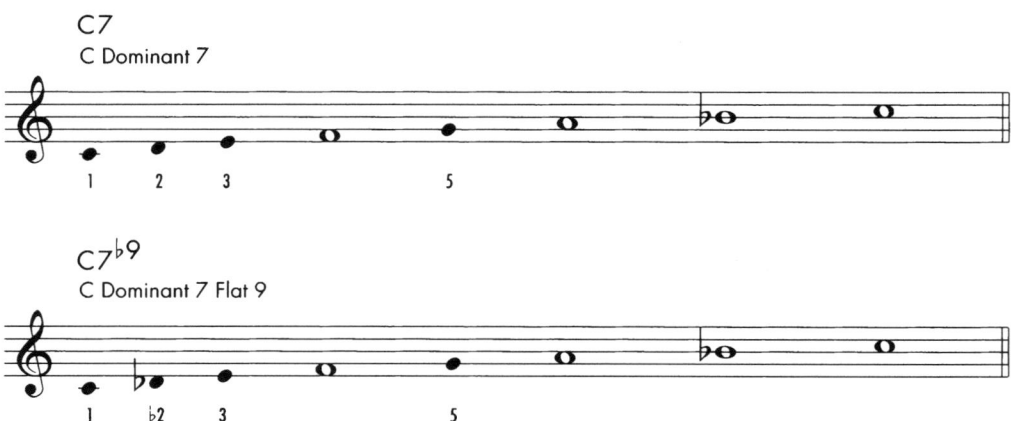

12

**Note that a Minor 7♭5 chord (ø) may also use a "natural 9".

APPLYING THE 1-5 GROUPING TO SOLOS

These four note melodies and their permutations can be used on chord changes for improvising. By applying them to a song, that is, plugging in a four note grouping per chord change, it becomes clear how they work. The following example illustrates what the first twelve bars of a common pattern of chord changes would sound like using the numbers 1-2-3-5, remembering that 1-2-3-5 is replaced by 1-3-4-5 on minor chords.

Example #1 (C Treble Clef Instruments)

I FOUR NOTE GROUPINGS 1-5

Example #1 (B♭ Instruments)

Example #1 (E♭ Instruments)

Example #1 (Bass Clef Instruments)

Don't be overwhelmed by the number of possible permutations. Once you feel comfortable with the basic grouping of 1-2-3-5, practicing one or two permutations from each column is sufficient. It isn't necessary to practice all 24 permutations as mastery of a few will enable you to incorporate others into your playing.

The following melody uses the permutation 3-5-2-1 on that same set of chord changes.

Example #2 (C Treble Clef Instruments)

Example #2 (B♭ Instruments)

Example #2 (E♭ Instruments)

Example #2 (Bass Clef Instruments)

For minor chords the permutation is 4-5-3-1; four of the minor replaces three of the major and three of the minor replaces two of the major.

| 3 | 5 | 2 | 1 | Major and Dominant |
| 4 | 5 | 3 | 1 | Minor |

The reason for replacing 3 of the major with 4 of the minor and 2 of the major with 3 of the minor is to keep the same contour or shape of the melody within the chordal movement.

Question: For the major permutation 2-1-5-3 , what is he corresponding minor permutation?

| 2 | 1 | 5 | 3 | Major and Dominant |
| ? | 1 | 5 | ? | Minor |

Answer: 3-1-5-4. Three of the minor replaces two of the major and four of the minor replaces three of the major.

FOUR NOTE GROUPINGS 1-5

Example #3 illustrates the permutation 2-1-5-3.

Example #3 (C Treble Clef Instruments)

Example #3 (B♭ Instruments)

Example #3 (E♭ Instruments)

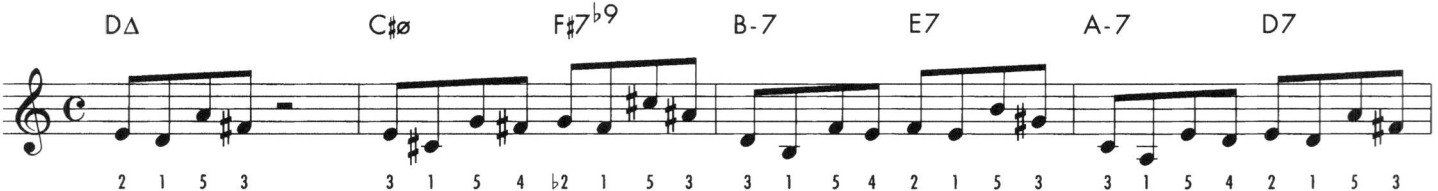

Example #3 (Bass Clef Instruments)

Playing these eighth note melodies through chord changes provides a pathway to lyrical and melodic improvisation as well as a method for practicing ear training. Hearing the sound of each chord and the color of each note is essential to musical development. Intellectually understanding or conceptualizing musical ideas helps the ear to categorize what it is hearing but knowing what something is in the mind is not a substitute for knowing what it sounds like. There is no substitute for the ear! Be sure to listen to what each note sounds like over the chord it is being played on.

The harmonic texture of these melodic segments is an integral part of all styles of jazz improvisation, from dixieland, to swing, to bebop, and beyond. What changes from style to style is the feel and sometimes the harmonic complexity. One approach to making these exercises sound more musical involves rhythmic variation and this technique called "editing" will be discussed in later lessons.

Learning to improvise takes time and patience. It is important that you learn the assigned lessons as future lessons will depend on your knowledge of prior ones. It is far better to learn one tune well rather than learning many tunes superficially.

ASSIGNMENT 1

1. Play the four note grouping 1-2-3-5 on Tune #1 or Tune #2 remembering to substitute 1-3-4-5 for the minor chords. Tune #1 is an easier selection, Tune #2 is more difficult.

2. Play three other permutations on the same tune; one that begins with 2, one that begins with 3, and one that begins with 5. You may find it helpful to write out the first four bars of "On The Brink" with each pattern.

   The following choices will give you a good variety of melodies to play and these are also permutations that are usually technically easy to play on most instruments.

For Major	**For Minor**
a) 2 - 1 - 5 - 3	3 - 1 - 5 - 4
b) 3 - 5 - 2 - 1	4 - 5 - 3 - 1
c) 5 - 3 - 2 - 1	5 - 4 - 3 - 1

TUNE #1 "LADY DUCK"

Concert Instruments

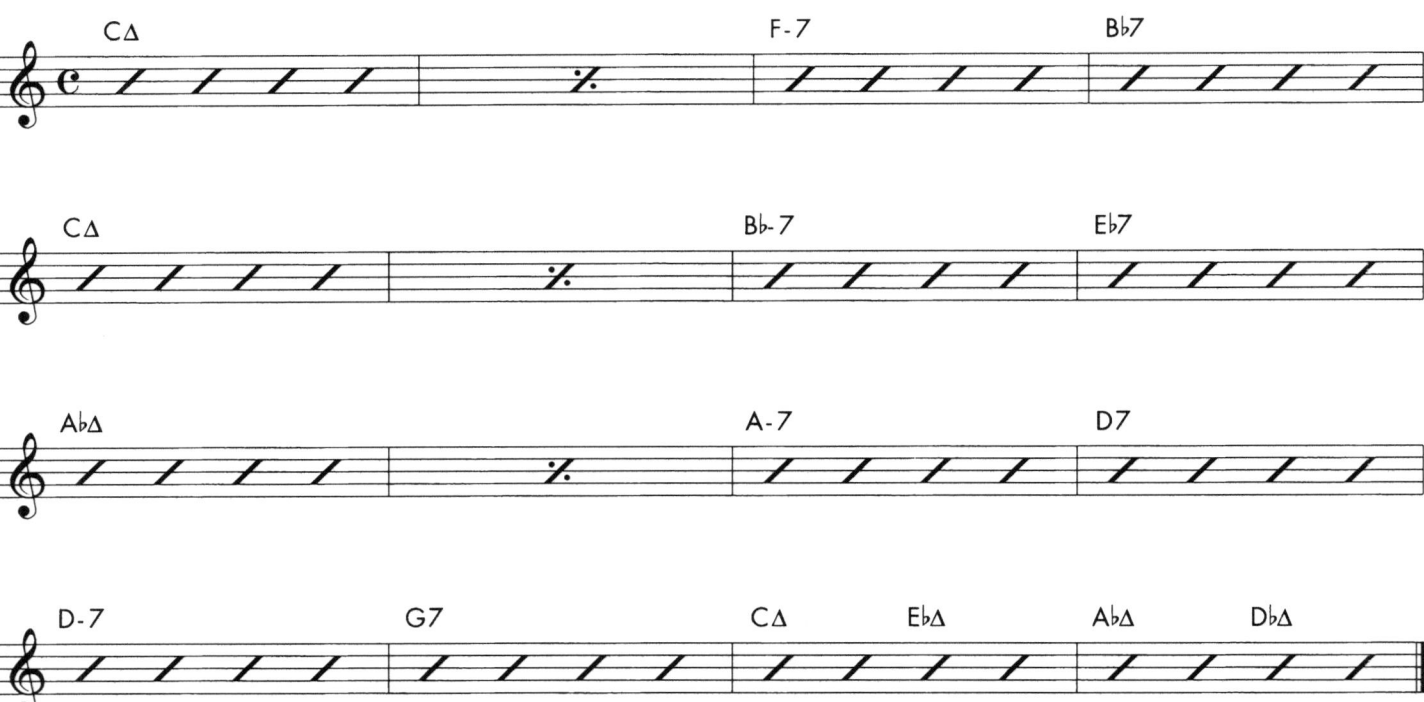

TUNE #1 "LADY DUCK"

B♭ Instruments

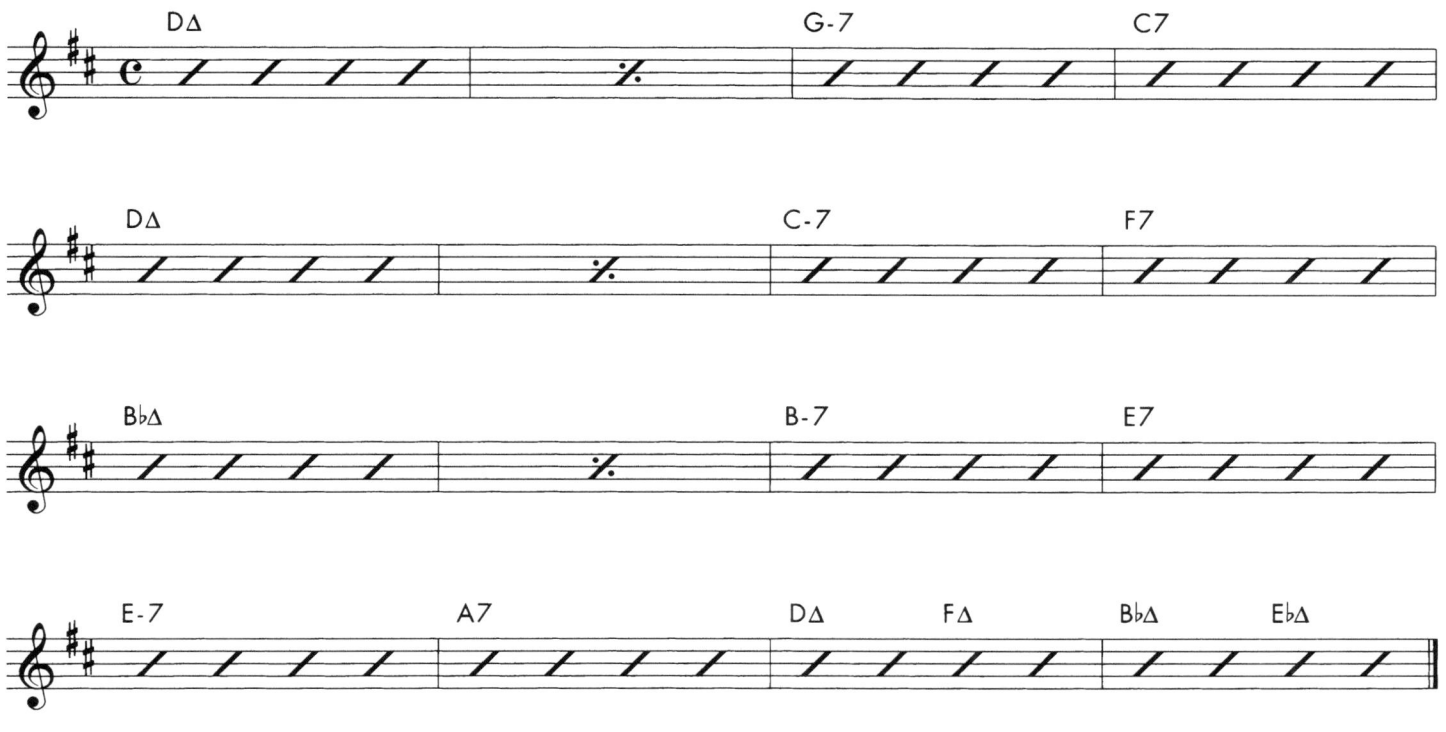

TUNE #1 "LADY DUCK"

E♭ Instruments

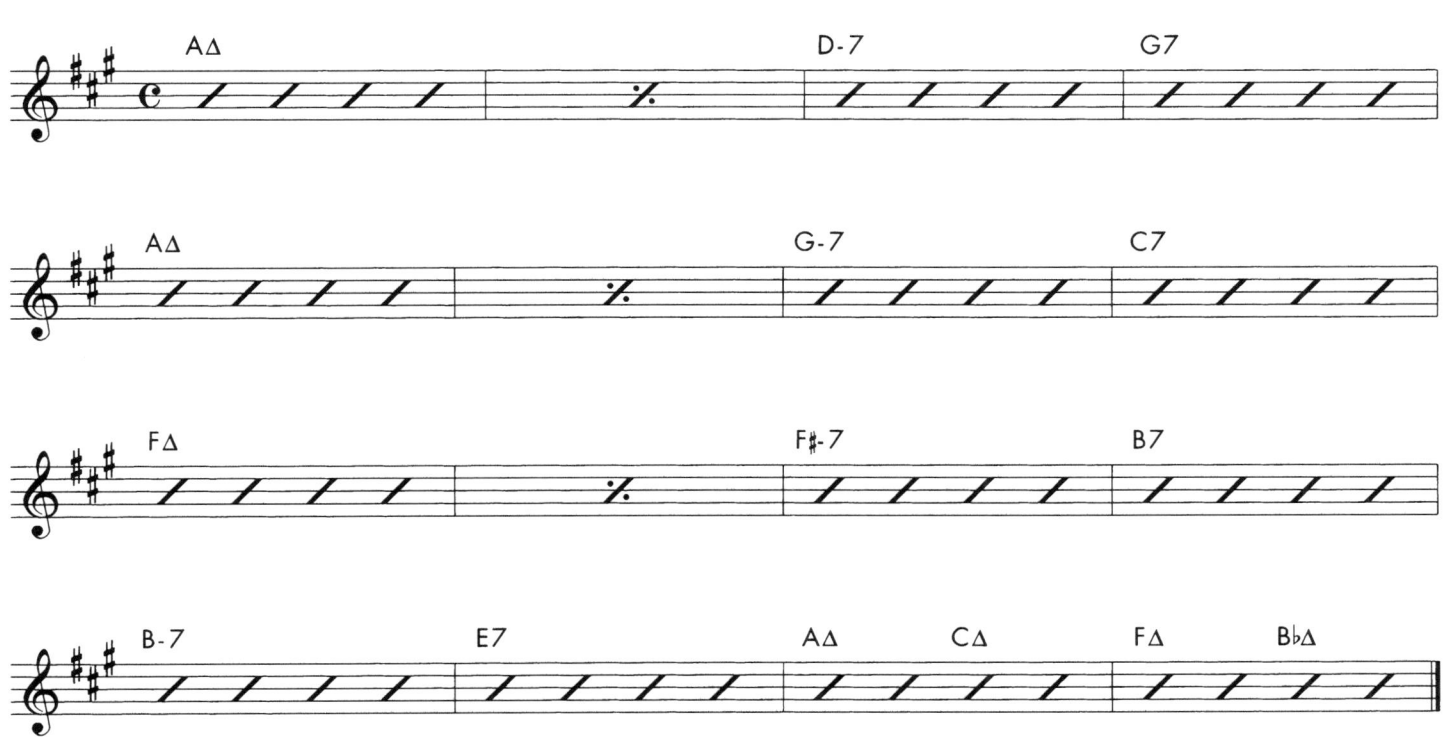

TUNE #2 "ON THE BRINK"

Concert Instruments

TUNE #2 "ON THE BRINK"

B♭ Instruments

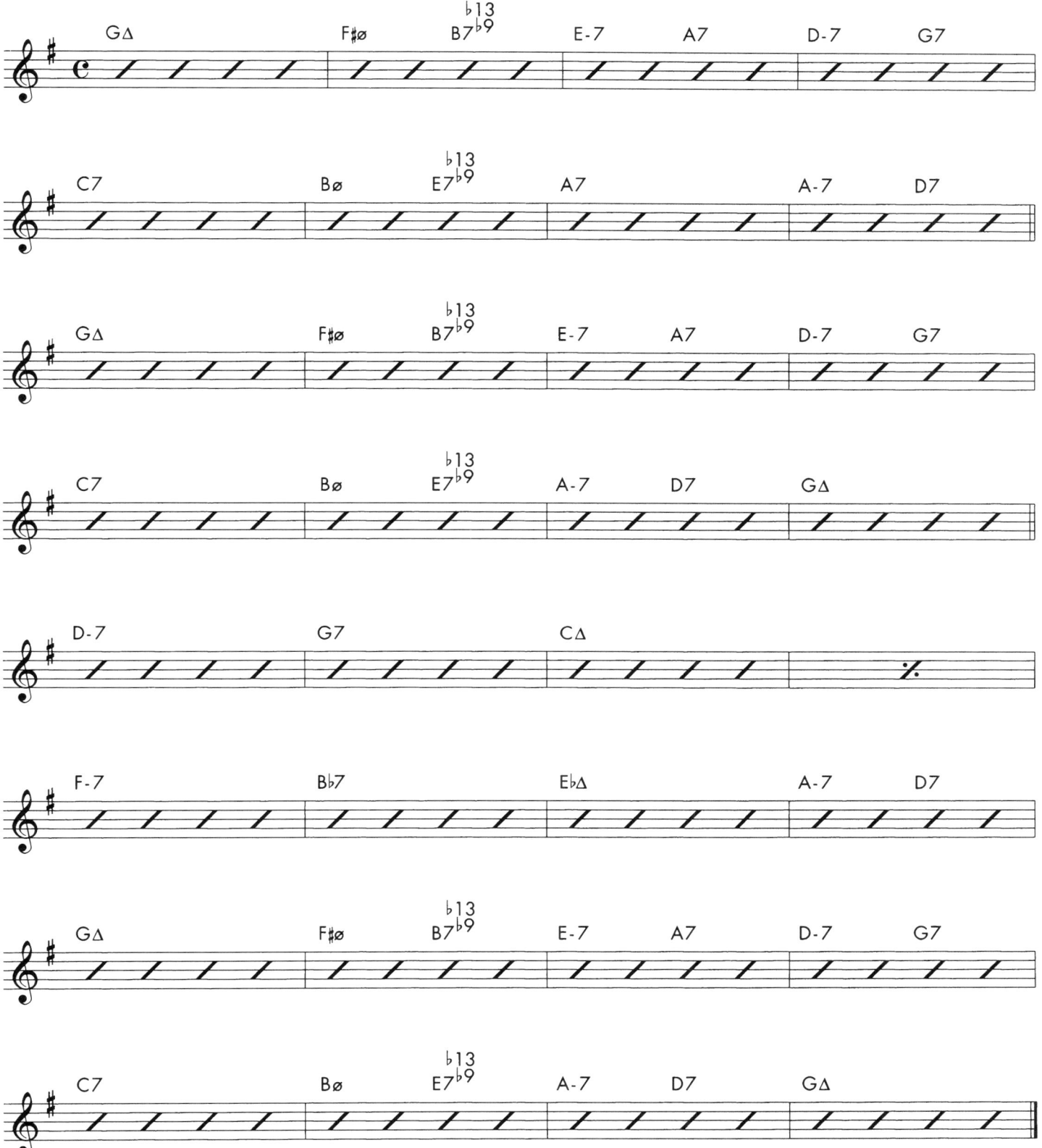

I FOUR NOTE GROUPINGS 1-5

TUNE #2 "ON THE BRINK"

E♭ Instruments

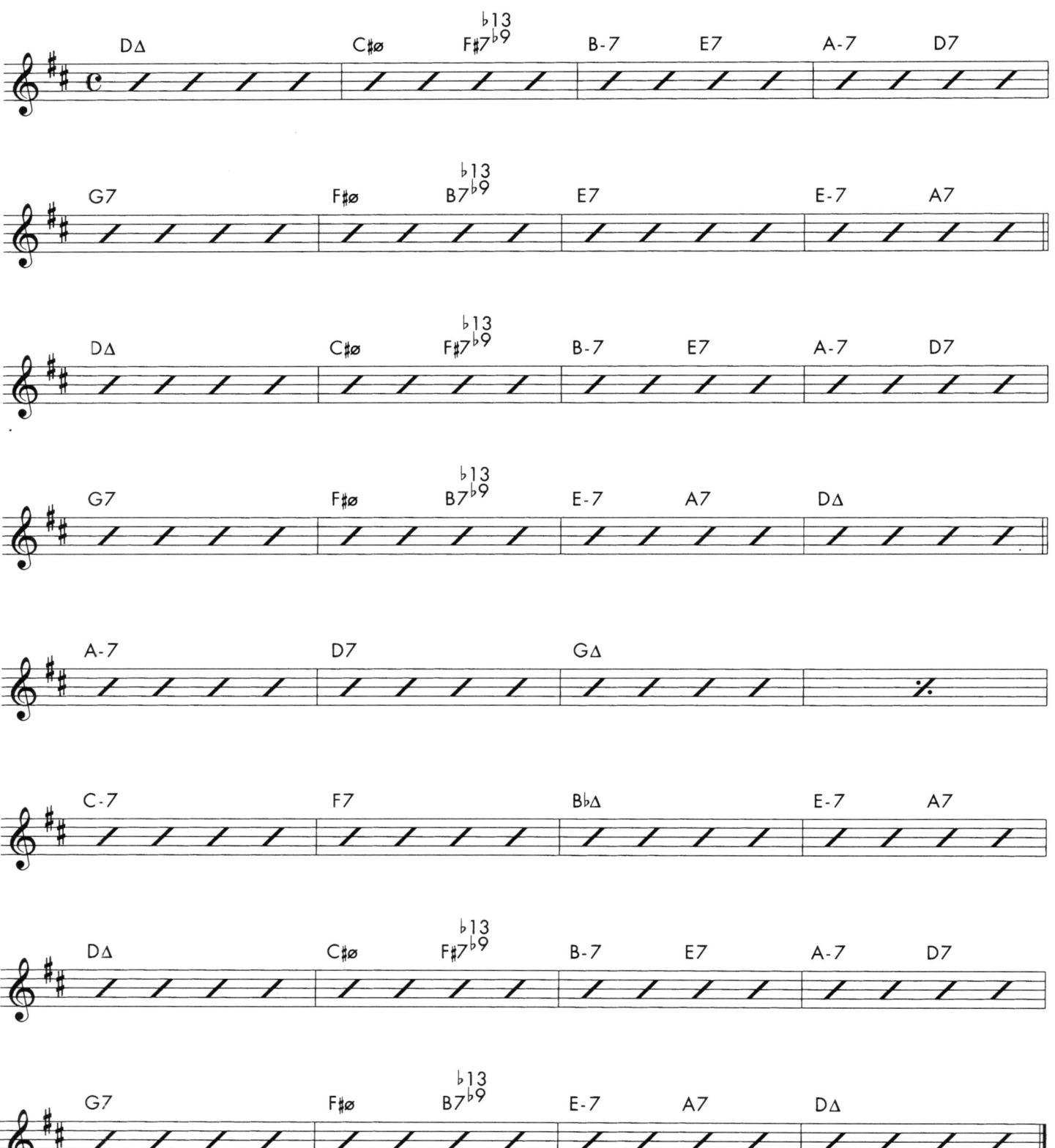

11 MIXING UP PERMUTATIONS

Once you have become familiar with four permutations from the 1-5 grouping, the next step is to play through a song and mix up these different permutations. The goal here is to strive for variety in your melodic lines.

Having memorized four permutations, you can then randomly arrange the notes in different shapes. It is very likely that you will begin to play permutations which you haven't even practiced simply by thinking about the different possible shapes of these four note melodies. The key word here is "shape".

The following example illustrates mixing up whatever permutations come to mind on the first eight bars of Tune #2.

Example #4 (C Treble Clef Instruments)

Example #4 (B♭ Instruments)

Example #4 (E♭ Instruments)

Example #4 (Bass Clef Instruments)

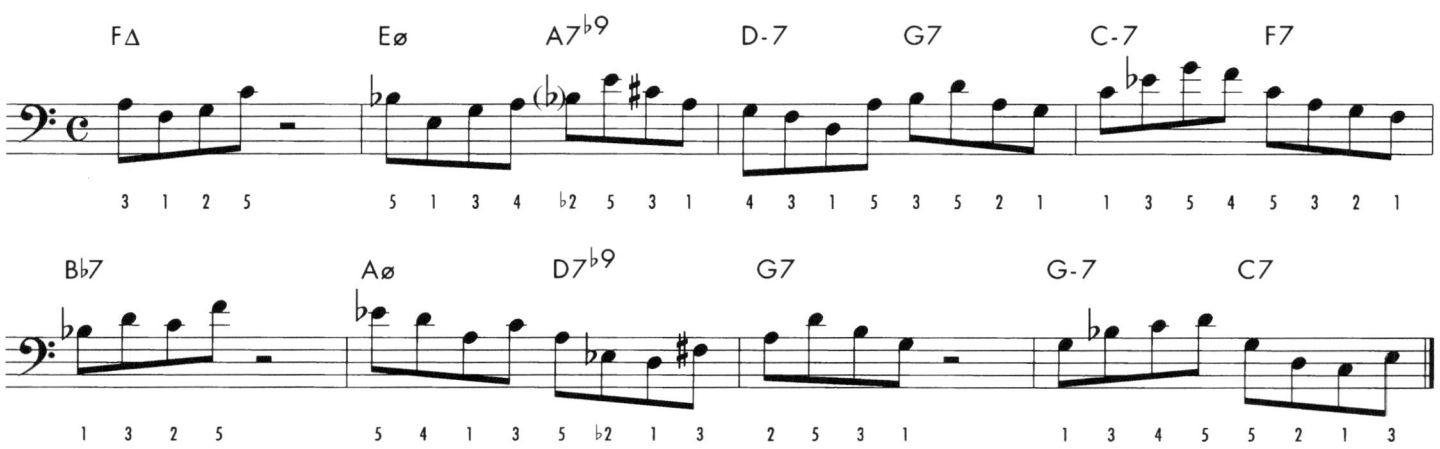

The most common pitfall students encounter when mixing up these patterns is avoiding the use of groupings starting with 2 or 3. Ascending 1-2-3-5 and descending 5-3-2-1 patterns tend to be overused as they are the most accessible melodies in the beginning. It is important to practice with patterns starting with the numbers 2 or 3 so that they may become as readily available to you as those beginning with 1 or 5.

ASSIGNMENT 11

1. Mix up any permutations randomly on Tune #1 (easier) or Tune #2 (more difficult). Chances are you will play the four you've practiced, however, try to play any shape that comes to mind as written in Example #4.

2. Practice four permutations of the 1 - 5 grouping on another song; Tune #3 for an easier selection, or Tune #4 for a more difficult one. Notice the difference in chord concentration between these two tunes. It's a good idea to practice tunes with many changes as it helps you to learn this system more quickly.

3. Mix up any permutation randomly on Tune #3 or Tune #4.

TUNE #3 "LUNAR"

Concert Instruments

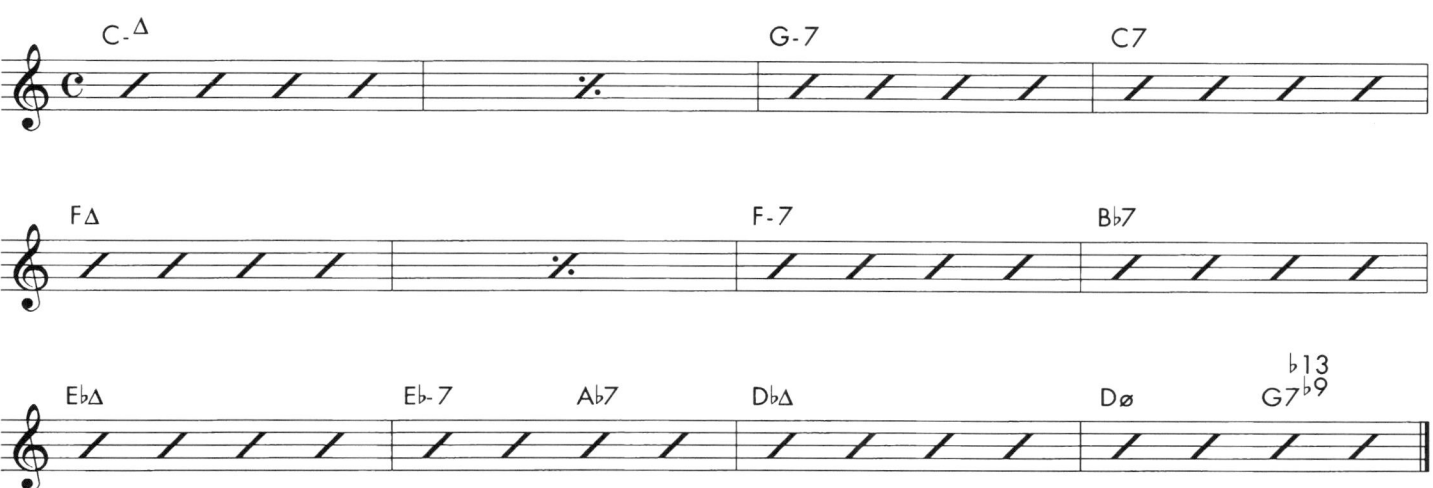

TUNE #3 "LUNAR"

B♭ Instruments

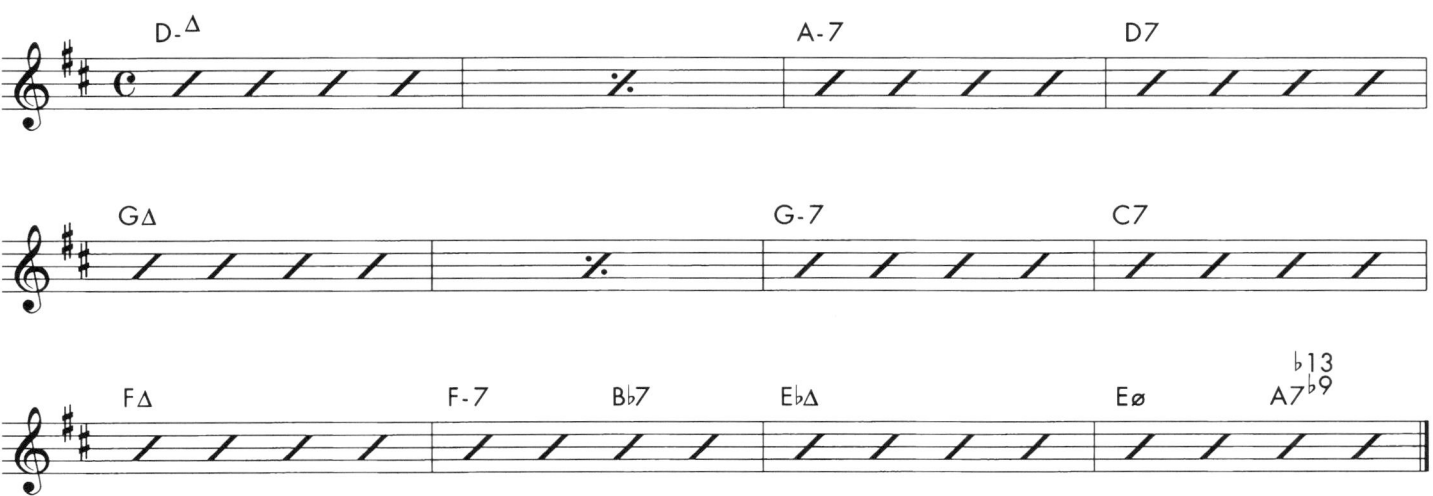

11 MIXING UP PERMUTATIONS

TUNE #3 "LUNAR"

E♭ Instruments

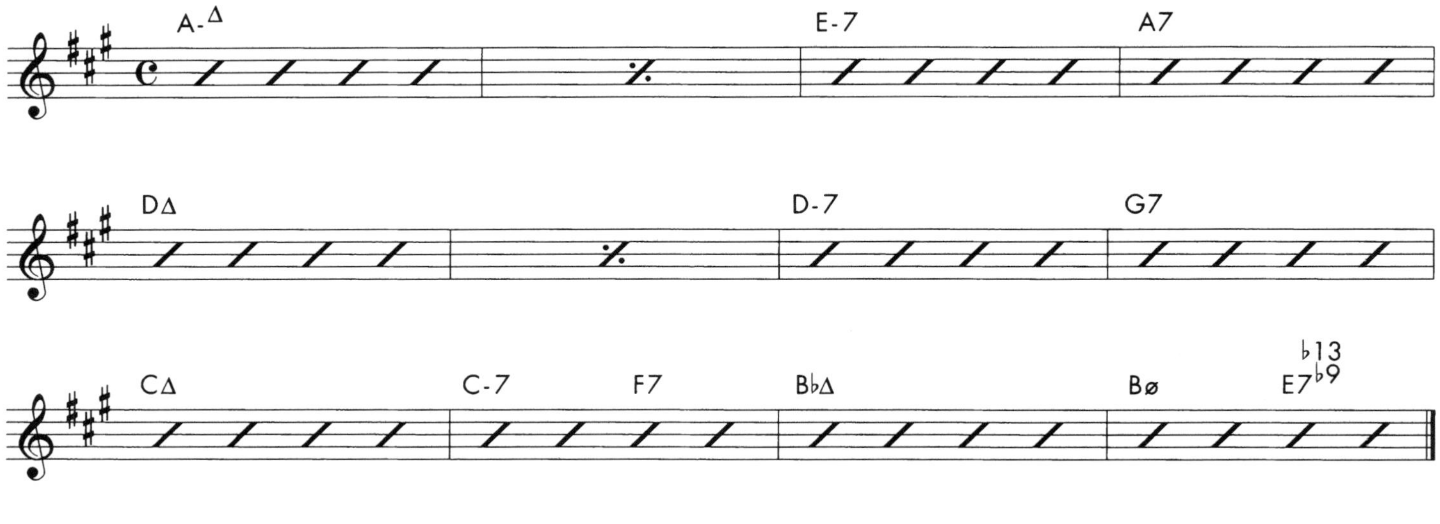

A-Δ		E-7	A7
D△		D-7	G7
C△	C-7 F7	B♭△	Bø E7♭9♭13

TUNE #4 "HOW LOW THE SUN"

Concert Instruments

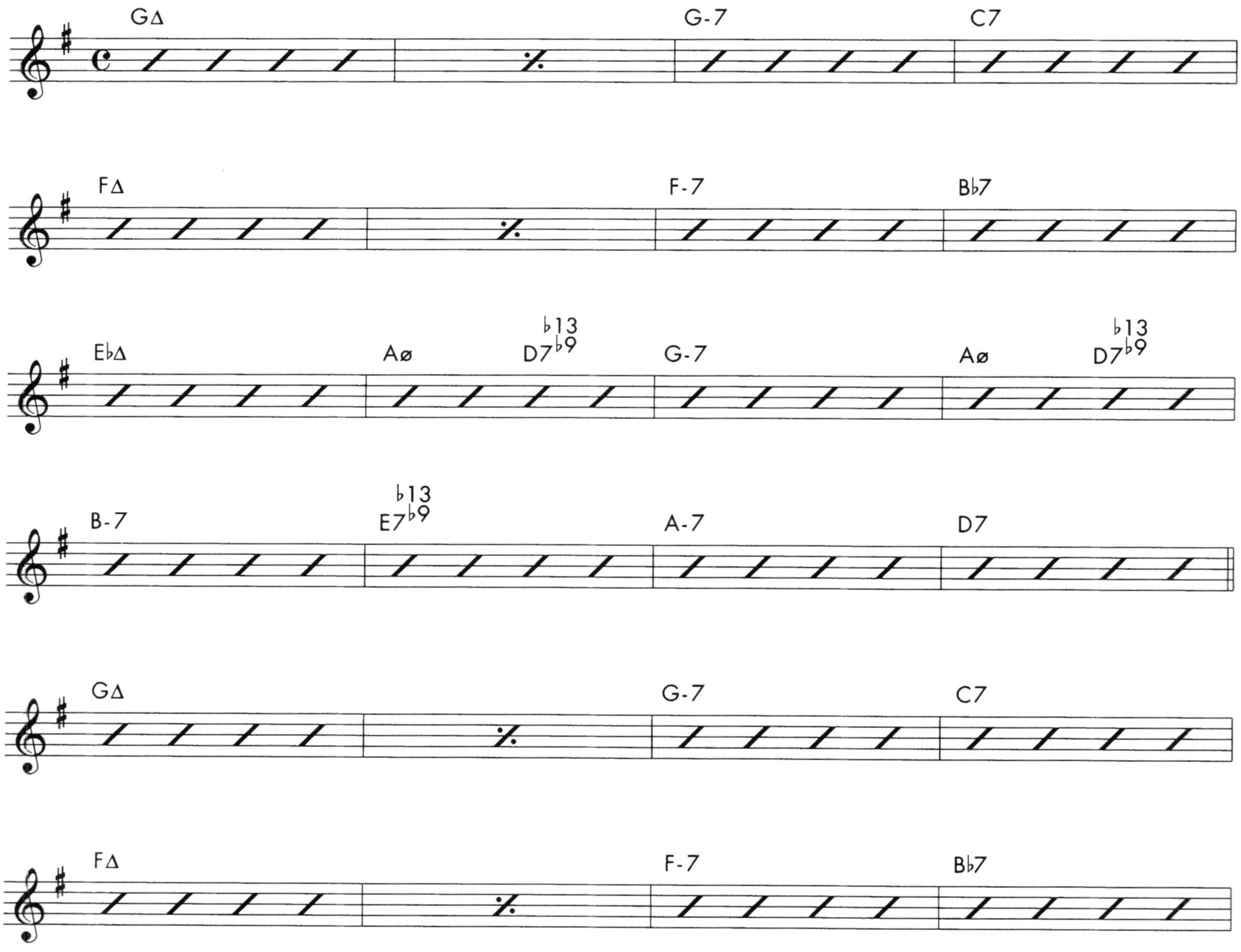

G△		G-7	C7
F△		F-7	B♭7
E♭△	Aø D7♭9♭13	G-7	Aø D7♭9♭13
B-7	E7♭9♭13	A-7	D7
G△		G-7	C7
F△		F-7	B♭7

28

11 MIXING UP PERMUTATIONS

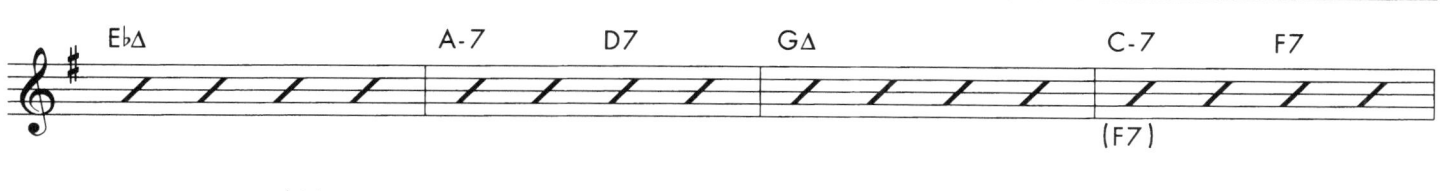

TUNE #4 "HOW LOW THE SUN"

B♭ Instruments

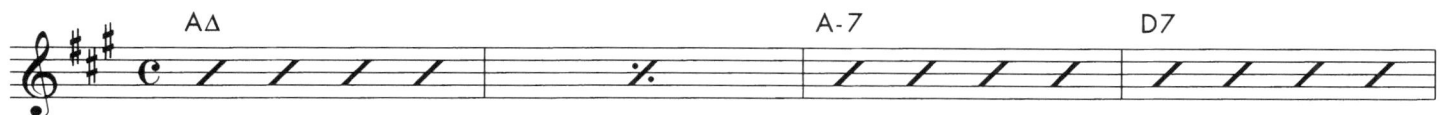

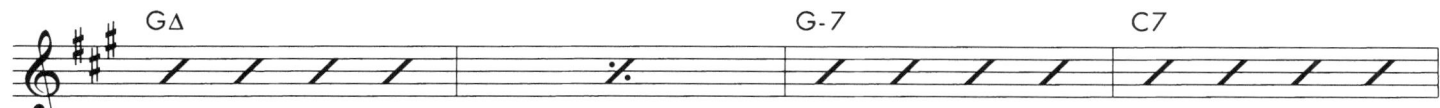

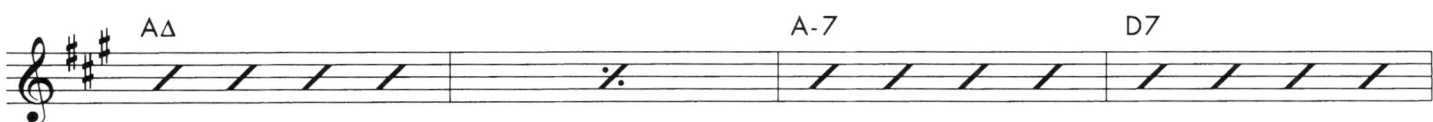

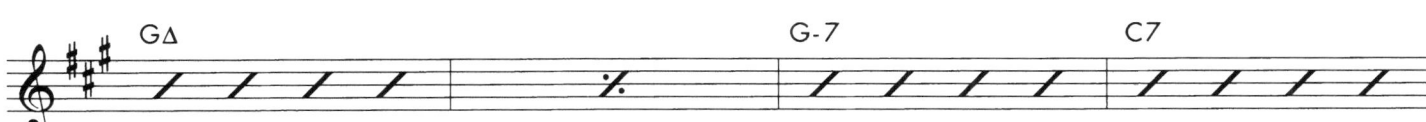

TUNE #4 "HOW LOW THE SUN"

E♭ Instruments

III VISUALIZATION

For a musician, visualization is the process of picturing in our mind's eye what we hear in our mind's ear.

Visualization is something we all do. In fact, putting a visual form before the mind's eye or forming a mental image is something that precedes most things that we do. Baseball players visualize the pitch that is about to come in anticipation of how they will swing. Basketball players visualize their moves both defensively and offensively. Lawyers visualize their legal arguements. Composers visualize their musical options. Jazz musicians visualize their improvisation.

Visualization speeds up the process of learning how to improvise.

How does one actually visualize? First, sit upright in a comfortable chair with your feet flat on the floor. Take a few deep breaths in order to relax, assume a relaxed mental and physical posture. Before the mind's eye, picture the notes of a C major scale. You have just visualized.

You might ask, how does one picture notes? How does one picture something intangible? It is by symbol that we give sound a visible form. For example, you could visualize the sound of the note "A" by at least three methods.

1. Imagine the letter A in your mind (not necessarily on a staff). Imagine what it sounds like.

2. Imagine that you are fingering the note A on your instrument.

3. Imagine that you are seeing the note A on a musical staff.

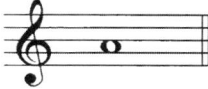

Many people may not be able to ascertain the exact pitch that they are imagining but it is not important at this time.

BLOCK CHORD VISUALIZATION

Maintaining a relaxed mental and physical posture, the first step is to visualize the changes of a tune in block chord fashion. See each chord or change as a whole rather than as four individual notes. For example, if the chord is F major, you would envision this picture:

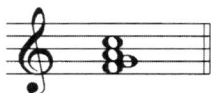

From this mental image of an F major chord, the individual notes F-G-A-C can then be arranged in any order. It is much easier to grab the melodic notes for each chord change when you already have the block chord picture in mind. The following is an example of how one would envision the first eight bars of Tune #2, "On The Brink".

LINEAR VISUALIZATION

The next step involves visualizing the chord progression in linear fashion, that is, with the block chord picture in mind, envision the individual eighth notes moving through the tune. Taking the first of the four note groupings practiced in Chapter I, 1-2-3-5 and 1-3-4-5, visualize in your mind, using one of the three methods previously described, that you are counting time and playing this melodic sequence through the song "On The Brink". You would think, not play Tune #2 "On The Brink" (page 33):

Visualize as slow as you wish at first because speed is not the issue. The process of visualization can also include sound. Try to hear the melodies as you visualize them.

The major stumbling block to making practice time effectual is most often a lack of concentration. It's very easy to get side-tracked by the sound of your instrument. One moment you might be working on a specific idea and minutes later you realize you've gone off on a tangent playing something else. When you practice visualization without your instrument it demands concentration.

Very often ten minutes of visualization is equivalent to two hours of physical practice.

THE PROCESS OF BODY TEACHING MIND?

The reason visualization is so valuable is because it reverses the process of the body teaching the mind. A student practices a particular grouping of notes over and over again untill the body actually memorizes the pattern. How many times has your body been playing an exercise by rote while your mind is off somewhere else? With the use of visualization the mind actually teaches the body and the mind remembers what the body is more apt to forget. The mind visualizes what the body does in a multi-dimensional fashion. It practices the fingerings and the notes, it hears the sound and the content, it feels the intention, the emotion, and the nuances of what is played. The body then follows suit. The body teaching the mind is actually a backward process and for this reason through the use of visualization we are able to learn more quickly.

Wherever you have a difficult time mentally is where you will encounter problems playing on your instrument. Work it out mentally and you will no longer have those problems. With practice, whatever you are able to visualize you will then be able to play.

TUNE #2 "ON THE BRINK"

III VISUALIZATION

ASSIGNMENT III

1. Visualize the changes to Tune #1 or Tune #2 in block chord fashion. Tune #1 is the easier of the two.

2. Visualize the four note grouping 1-2-3-5 through the tune you have chosen.

3. Visualize the same tune using different permutations.

4. Visualize the same tune mixing up whatever patterns come to mind from the block chord picture.

5. Repeat steps 1 through 4 on either Tune #3 (easier) or Tune #5 (more difficult).

6. After practicing visualizing on Tune #5, try improvising on the tune with your instrument and notice if the process has helped you.

TUNE #5 "INSIDE THE MILKY WAY"

Concert Instruments

34

III VISUALIZATION

TUNE #5 "INSIDE THE MILKY WAY"

B♭ Instruments

TUNE #5 "INSIDE THE MILKY WAY"

E♭ Instruments

IV THE CREATIVE IMAGINATION

Imagine what a trumpet sounds like. A saxophone. A guitar. A piano.

Imagine what a high note sounds like. A low note.

Imagine what the note "A" sounds like on your instrument. Yes, most will say that they are not able to hear the note, but just imagine it. In time many will be able to hear the pitch although it doesn't matter if you cannot.

Picture what a particular melody sounds like. Give it a shape in your mind's eye.

Take a set of chord changes and with the notes that we've practiced and visualized improvise a solo. Improvise melodies using your creative imagination. Far fetched? No! It is a normal process for the creative artist to first imagine his or her sound.

In a sense, it is like taking the process of visualization one step further into the realm of creativity. For example, have you ever noticed that hearing a great player often helps your own playing to improve? It is because we internalize or take into our imagination how they sound and that in turn effects the way we sound.

Imagine what you would like your music to sound like, what you would like it to feel like; the clearer the picture in your mind the closer to physical reality your product will be.

The creative imagination extends into all areas of our lives. It enables us to bring to ourselves that which we desire. It is necessary to envision our goals because what we desire takes place in our inner worlds first. So, why not picture yourself getting a good sound, having fun playing music, and achieving the ends which you desire?

ASSIGNMENT IV

1. Create your inner space. Once again, sit comfortably, take a few deep breaths, stop the mind, stop the world, and surround yourself with positive energy.

2. Imagine how you like to play, how you would like to sound.

3. See yourself achieving that sound and being fulfilled playing music.

Remember that very often our goals are long range goals and that it is necessary to visualize shorter range goals or smaller steps leading to that end result.

V EDITING

Up until this point in our numerical approach to improvisation we have been playing four notes to each chord change. This approach has resulted in predominantly eighth note solos making the music sound slightly mechanical and too much like an exercise. In order to achieve more variety and to get away from this exercise like sound, we are simply going to leave some of the notes out. From the original groupings we can now select or omit one, two, three, or four of the notes for each chord. This technique, called "editing", provides the missing rhythmic variety to our eighth note solos.

An eighth note melody without editing:

That same melody after editing:

While in the above example there are two chord changes per bar, note that the use of editing is also very effective when the tune involves less harmonic movement, that is, when there is one chord for two, four, or even eight bars at a time. Even given the choice of 24 different permutations, playing continual eighth note patterns could sound one dimensional. The process of editing, or of sounding different rhythms, lends variety.

The following example illustrates the use of editing on a G major chord over four bars.

Before editing:

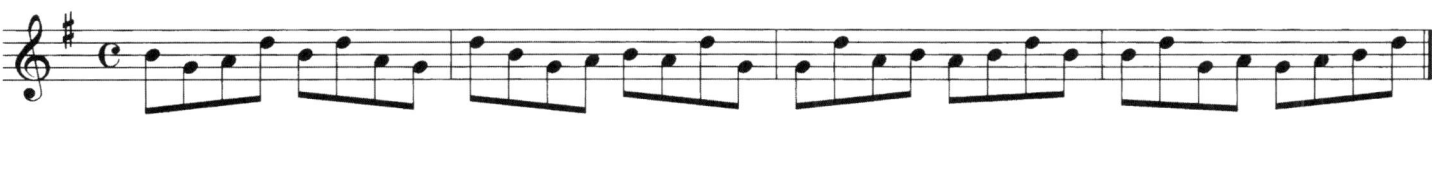

After editing:

V EDITING

Another editing option is the use of repeated notes.

Thus, the result of editing is to change the somewhat mechanical sounding eighth note rhythms into more musical melodies and motifs. Rhythmic variation is a much more expansive improvisational tool as the possibilities are infinite when compared with the choice of notes which we are keeping very finite by the numbering system. It is extremely helpful to listen to your favorite players and try to determine what kinds of rhythms they are employing. Listen for the spaces they leave! The silence in spaces is a solo unto itself. Take notice of how they are editing their solos. For example, where do their phrases begin and end, on or off the beat and on or off what beat?

The following is an example of an edited solo on a bebop blues.

Example #5 (C Treble Clef Instruments)

Example #5 (B♭ Instruments)

Example #5 (E♭ Instruments)

V EDITING

Example #5 (Bass Clef Instruments)

ASSIGNMENT V

1. Try writing out several edited solos on a few different tunes.

2. Try playing edited solos on these tunes using various rhythms. Remember that you can use repeated notes.

VI KEY CENTERS

The purpose of this chapter is to give some consideration to improvising on chord progressions that move through multiple key centers as well as those that remain in one tonal area for an extended number of bars. Years ago, standard tunes most often hovered around one key center unlike some of the songs of today which employ far more frequent modulations. In the past it was an easier task for the musician to anticipate the harmonic movement of a tune. For example, going up a major third or a fourth on the bridge was a common progression. On the other hand, the modern harmony of today's music might involve a chord sequence that moves through as many as three keys within just three bars. The modern player encounters a different situation in his or her improvisation.

SONGS WITH MULTIPLE KEY CENTERS

Applying the number system to more complex chord progressions can be extremely valuable as it allows one to capture the sound or quality of each chord change while giving the improvisor something very tangible to play. For example, given the chord progression:

The improvisor must play through three tonal areas (E♭, B and G) within four bars. Because the chord progression is complex, it sounds fine to play something simple yet concrete. Applying the four note groupings to these changes lends a kind of forward motion to the sound; the changes "play themselves".

One only needs to play simple melodies on each change in this type of progression. Within a more complex harmonic structure you cannot improvise in one key center and sound right. There is no all purpose scale that can be played throughout the changes. Each chord must be played one by one. There are many tunes with constantly changing key centers and playing the numbers will help you to get a handle on them.

SINGLE TONAL AREAS

The song which involves few chord changes presents yet another challenge and the way in which one approaches improvising on them is quite different from the technique we have just discussed. Given one chord for two, four, or eight bars at a time, it becomes necessary to vary the permutations or melodies.

The following example demonstrates how by varying permutations of the 1-2-3-5 grouping an interesting melody can be created on a G major chord over four bars.

This second example also employs the technique of editing.

Both songs with more or less harmonic complexity present the improvisor with a particular challenge and the numbering system provides a method for dealing with either situation.

ASSIGNMENT VI

1. Practice four different permutations on Tune #6 using one grouping that begins with 1, one that begins with 2, one that begins with 3, and one that begins with 5.

2. Practice playing through this same tune varying any permutations randomly. Think shapes. When mixing up the permutations, visualizing the block chords helps to put the notes at your fingertips. Also, try adding the technique of editing.

3. Repeat the above steps on Tune #4.

TUNE #6 "BRONTOSAURUS WALK"

Concert Instruments

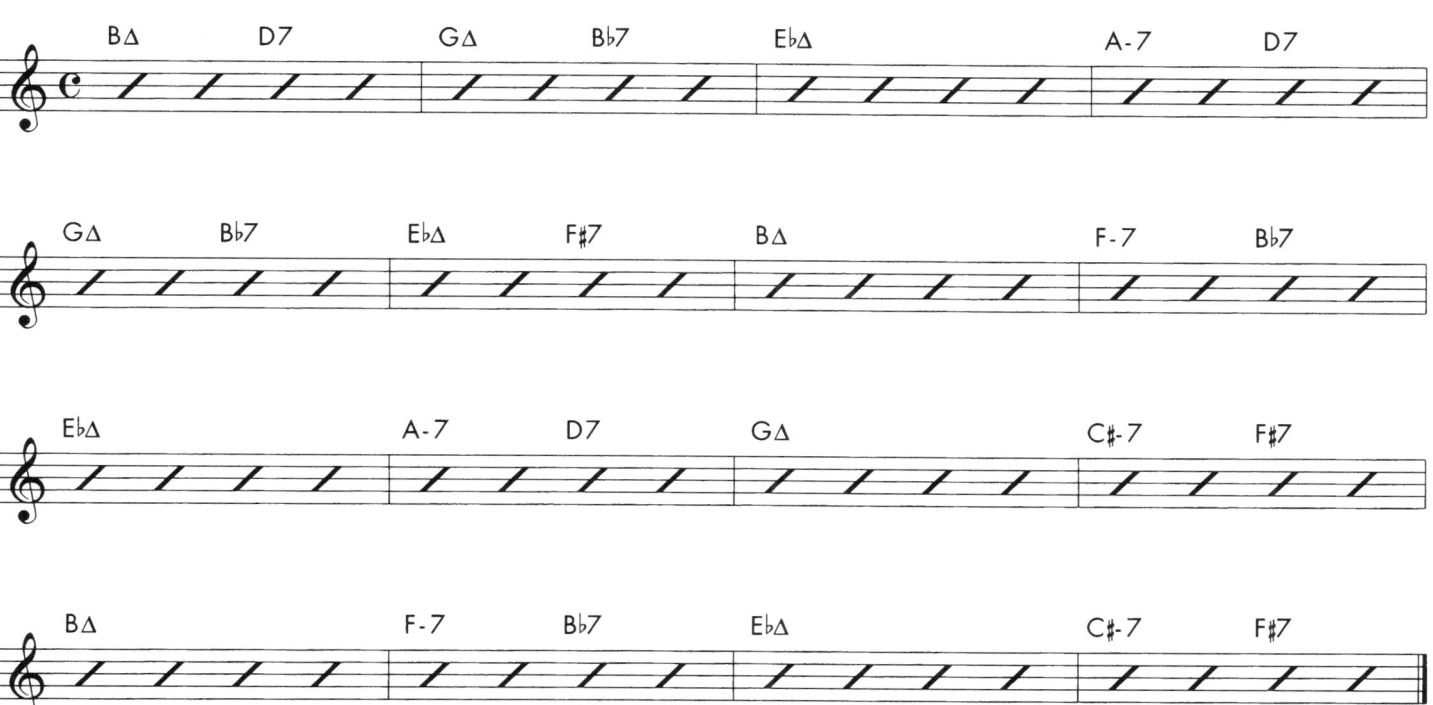

VI KEY CENTERS

TUNE #6 "BRONTOSAURUS WALK"

B♭ Instruments

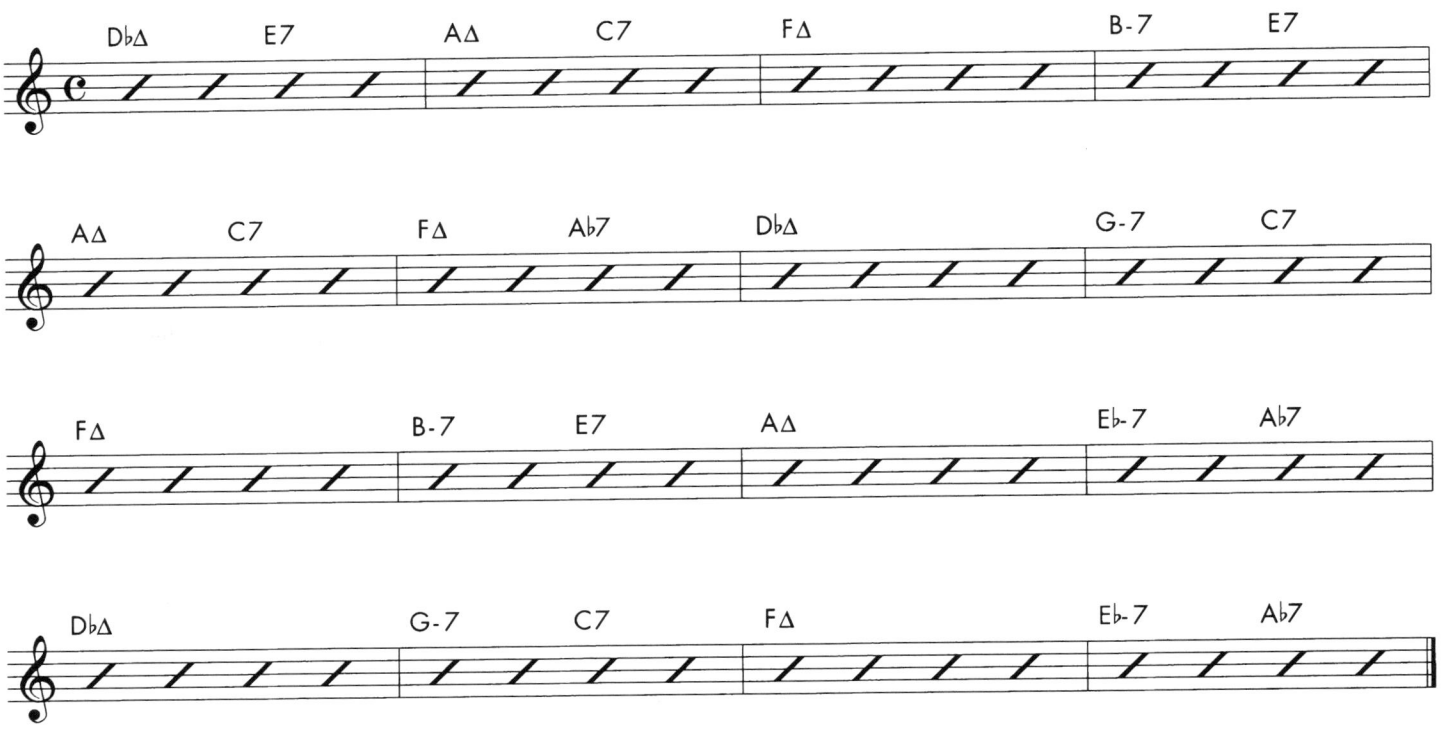

TUNE #6 "BRONTOSAURUS WALK"

E♭ Instruments

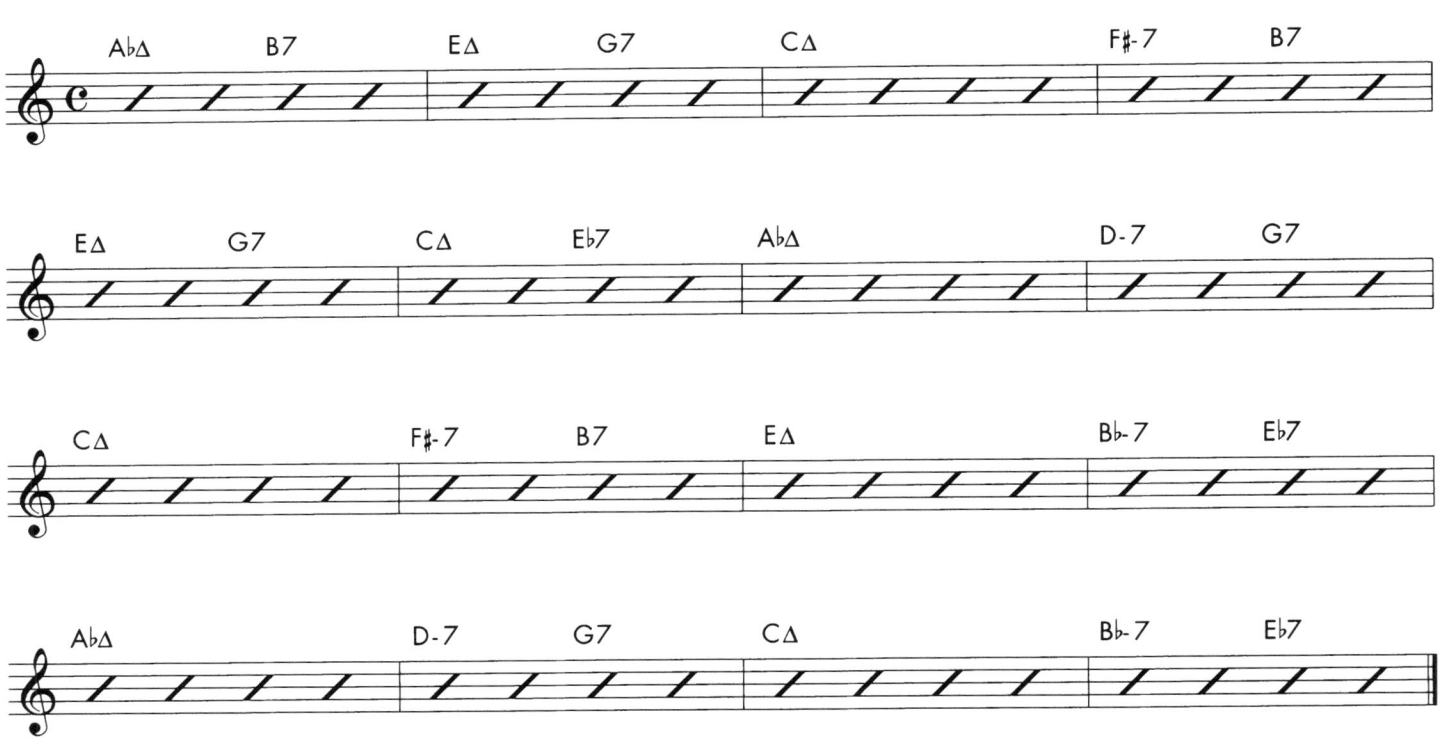

VII INVERSIONS

In Chapter III the concept of visualizing in block chord fashion was introduced. Given a chord, such as C major 7, we can visualize it and spell it in four different ways. The first way is the most common; it is spelled C-E-G-B with the C on the bottom and is called "root position". The notes can then be arranged in different orders by making each note the lowest tone and then building upwards from that point. These arrangements are called "inversions".

CHORDAL INVERSIONS

To make the first inversion of a C major 7 chord you take the root "C" and put it on top making the third of the chord "E" the lowest tone. Repeating this process, it follows that the second inversion would make "G" the lowest tone and the third inversion makes "B" the lowest tone.

C Major 7

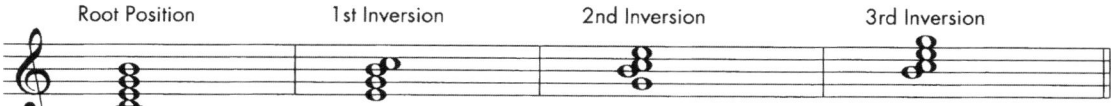

Written numerically, these inversions are:

Root Position   =   1 3 5 7
1st Inversion   =   3 5 7 1
2nd Inversion   =   5 7 3 1
3rd Inversion   =   7 1 3 5

LINEAR INVERSIONS

Similarly, given a C major chord, we can visualize the four note grouping 1-2-3-5 and spell it in four different ways. Each inversion of this grouping makes a different note the lowest tone.

C Major 1 - 2 - 3 - 5

Root Position   =   C D E G   ("C" is the lowest tone, building upwards)
1st Inversion   =   D E G C   ("D" is the lowest tone)
2nd Inversion   =   E G C D   ("E" is the lowest tone)
3rd Inversion   =   G C D E   ("G" is the lowest tone)

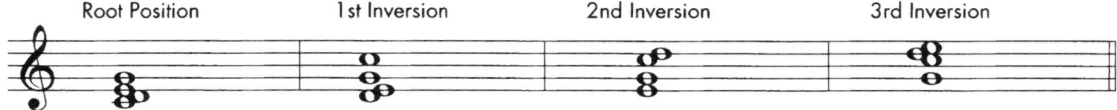

VII INVERSIONS

Applying inversions to the four note grouping 1-2-3-5 allows an even greater variety of shapes to these melodic lines.

Example: Four inversions of 2-1-5-3 on a C major chord.

Each of the 24 permutations of 1-2-3-5 can be played in four inversions giving us a total of 96 melodies in all. Don't get overwhelmed! If you can play the material in the previous chapters, then it is sufficient to practice one permutation with 1st inversion, one permutation with 2nd inversion, and one permutation with 3rd inversion. Why only one?

It is likely that if you have been visualizing, practicing one permutation will enable you to see that inversion as a block chord and you will then be able to play random patterns from it. These inversions come about very naturally and some won't even have to practice them at all.

ASSIGNMENT VII

1. Play the following permutations on Tune #1 or Tune #2:

   a) 5 - 1 - 3 - 2 in 1st inversion.

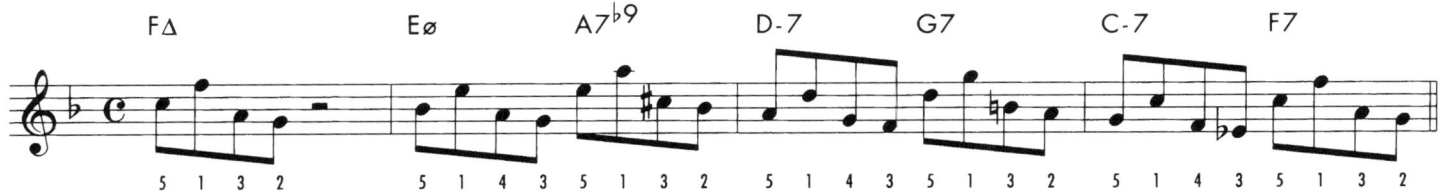

   b) 2 - 1 - 5 - 3 in 2nd inversion.

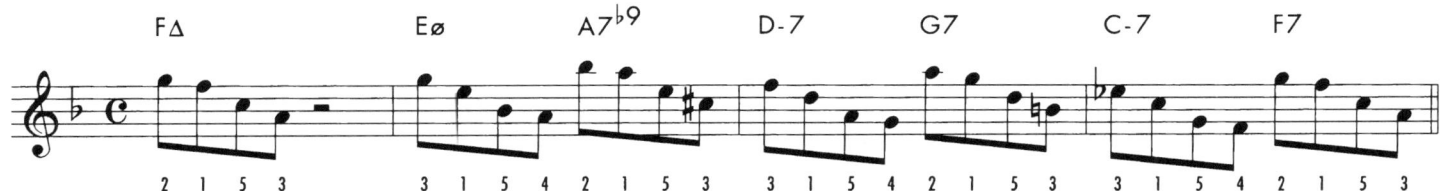

   c) 3 - 1 - 2 - 5 in 3rd inversion.

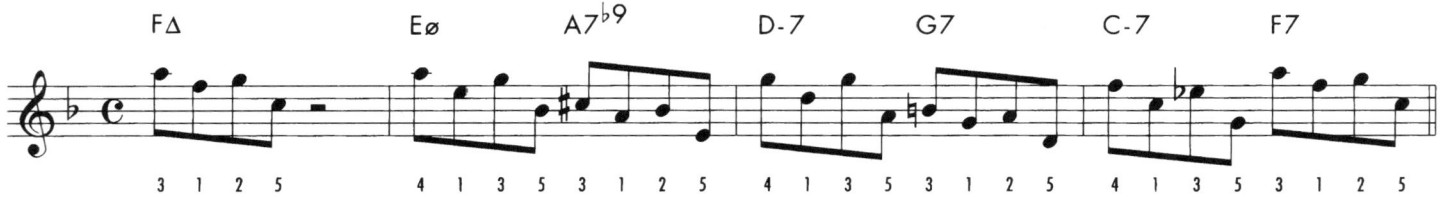

   The first four bars on Tune #2 are written out with each above permutation and inversion to help you get started.

2. Repeat the above exercise on Tune #3 or Tune #4.

3. Mix permutations and inversions while editing on Tune #2.

VIII PRACTICE EXERCISES

This chapter describes a series of exercises which will help you to master these number permutations to the point of accessibility in all harmonic situations in all tunes. There are four cycles or patterns to practice, giving a total of 48 chords; one cycle for major (which is also applicable to dominant chords), one cycle for minor, one for minor 7 flat 5, and in addition to these, one cycle for dominant 7 flat 9. Remember that "flat 9" is the same as "flat 2".

The order of each chord cycle is designed to make one think!

MAJOR CYCLE

Starting with the majors, first play or visualize the 1-2-3-5 grouping on the following chord pattern:

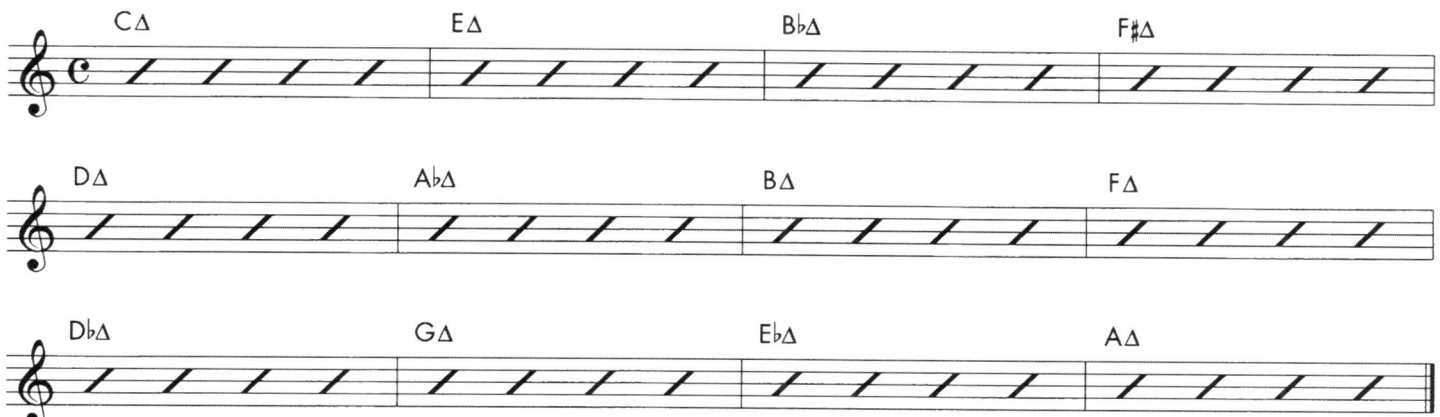

Next play through this same pattern using the permutation 2-1-5-3; then 3-5-2-1; and finally 5-3-2-1. When practicing this cycle, keep in mind that the numbers 1-2-3-5 also fit on dominant chords.

DOMINANT 7 FLAT 9 CYCLE

The next step is to play through or visualize the four note grouping

1-♭2-3-5 on the following dominant 7♭9 chord sequence.

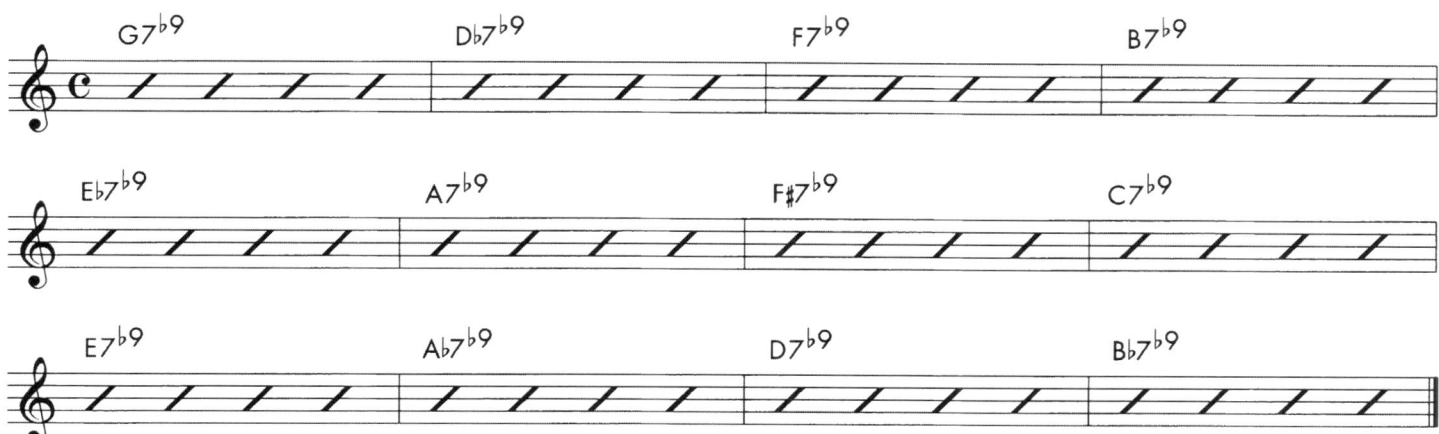

Repeat the process again using ♭2-1-5-3, then 3-5-♭2-1, and finally 5-3-♭2-1.

VIII PRACTICE EXERCISES

MINOR CYCLE

Next, think or play 1-3-4-5 on the following series of minor 7 chords:

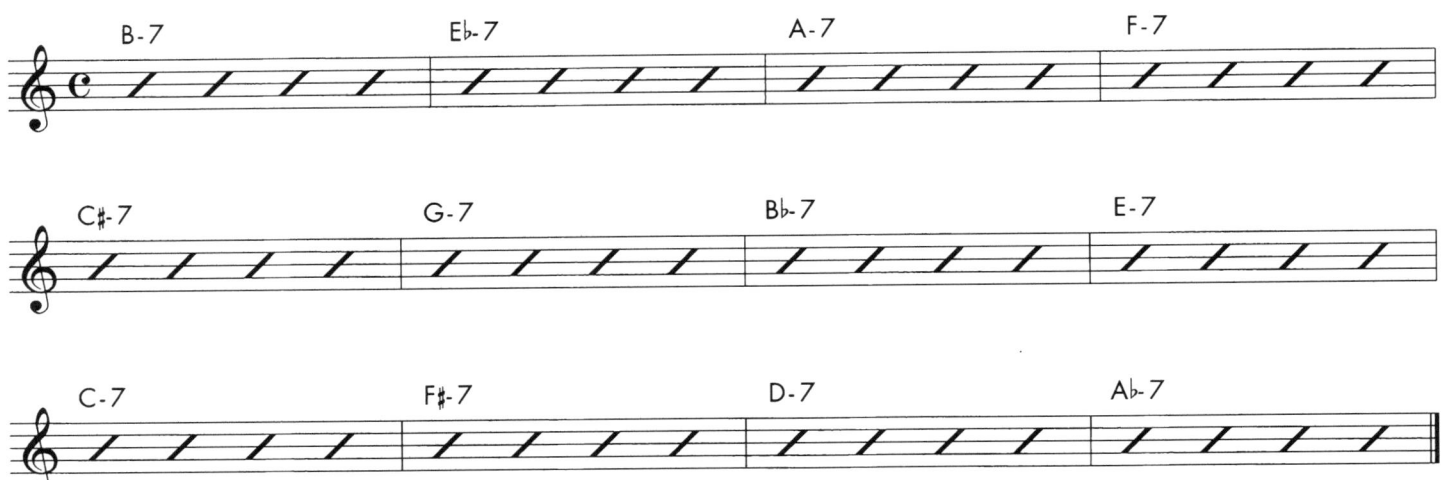

Again, play or think through the permutations: 3-1-5-4, 4-5-3-1, and 5-4-3-1, one at a time.

MINOR 7 FLAT 5 CYCLE

Finally, play or visualize 1-3-4-♭5 on the following pattern for minor 7 flat 5 chords:

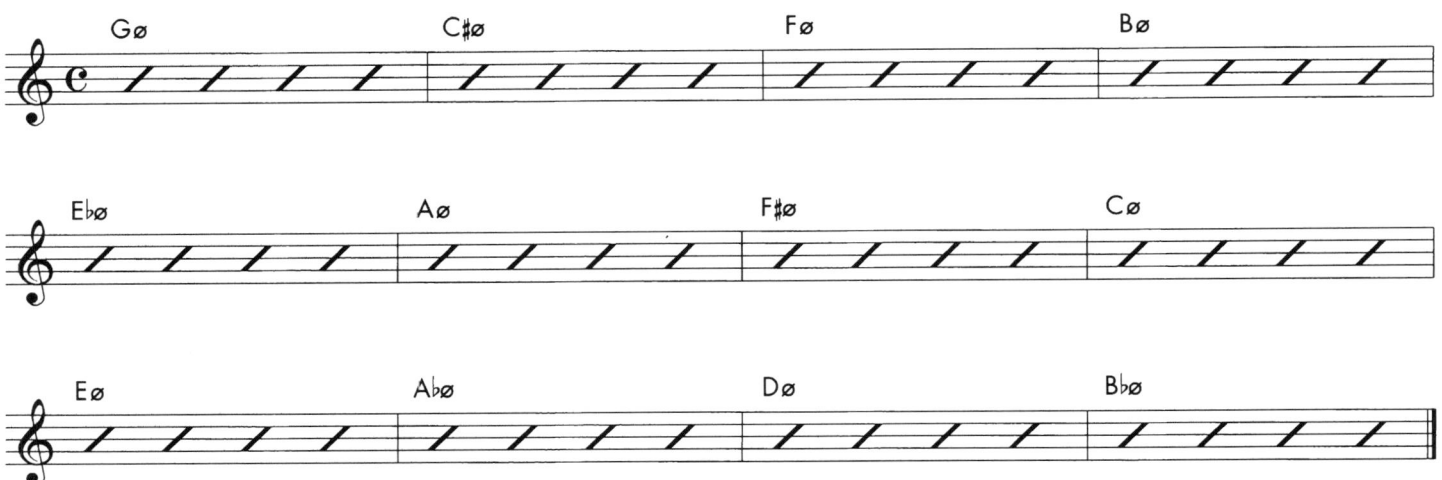

Repeat the cycle using 3-1-♭5-4, then 4-♭5-3-1, and ♭5-4-3-1.

Try practicing some inversions to the chord cycles.

When you first begin to think through this material it may take you a considerable amount of time but with continued practice on a daily basis the exercise can be completed in ten minutes or for some, less than five. These chords make up 95% of all the changes in tunes.

Again, if you are having trouble with certain permutations or a given set of chord changes, think it through. Visualization is extremely helpful. Also, you can substitute any groupings of notes discussed in later chapters on this exercise. Whatever the grouping of notes you are practicing, keep in mind that playing these numbers on chord changes is an excellent way to get the basic sound of the chord in your ear

REVIEW SKILLS

1. Do you know four permutations of the grouping 1-2-3-5 and 1-3-4-5?

2. Can you apply them to the songs you have worked on?

3. Have you been visualizing for 10 - 15% of your practice time?

4. Can you mix up the numbers randomly in order to obtain variety in the shape of your melodic lines?

5. Can you edit comfortably?

6. Can you use different inversions in your improvisations?

If you are not comfortable with any of the previous steps then keep working at it!

Tunes #7 and #8 are additional songs to work with.

THE LAW OF LIMITATION

"Plan your work and work your plan"

The amount of work planned is up to the individual. What you should aim for is to really complete one tune as opposed to dabbling in ten. If you can experience the previous chapters on one tune, you will be able to transfer what you have learned to any tune.

Learn one step at a time. Many students with the desire to improve right away want to move more quickly than they should. These students only scratch the surface and never master each step to the point where they are comfortable with them. Only those who are comfortable with the basics can fully develop the ongoing chapters.

Everyday you practice try and learn one thing completely as opposed to ten incompletely. Really learn it.

VIII PRACTICE EXERCISES

TUNE #7 "LOVERS AGAIN"

Concert Instruments

VIII PRACTICE EXERCISES

TUNE #7 "LOVERS AGAIN"

B♭ Instruments

VIII PRACTICE EXERCISES

TUNE #7 "LOVERS AGAIN"

E♭ Instruments

VIII PRACTICE EXERCISES

TUNE #8 "YOU'RE THE ONE"

Concert Instruments

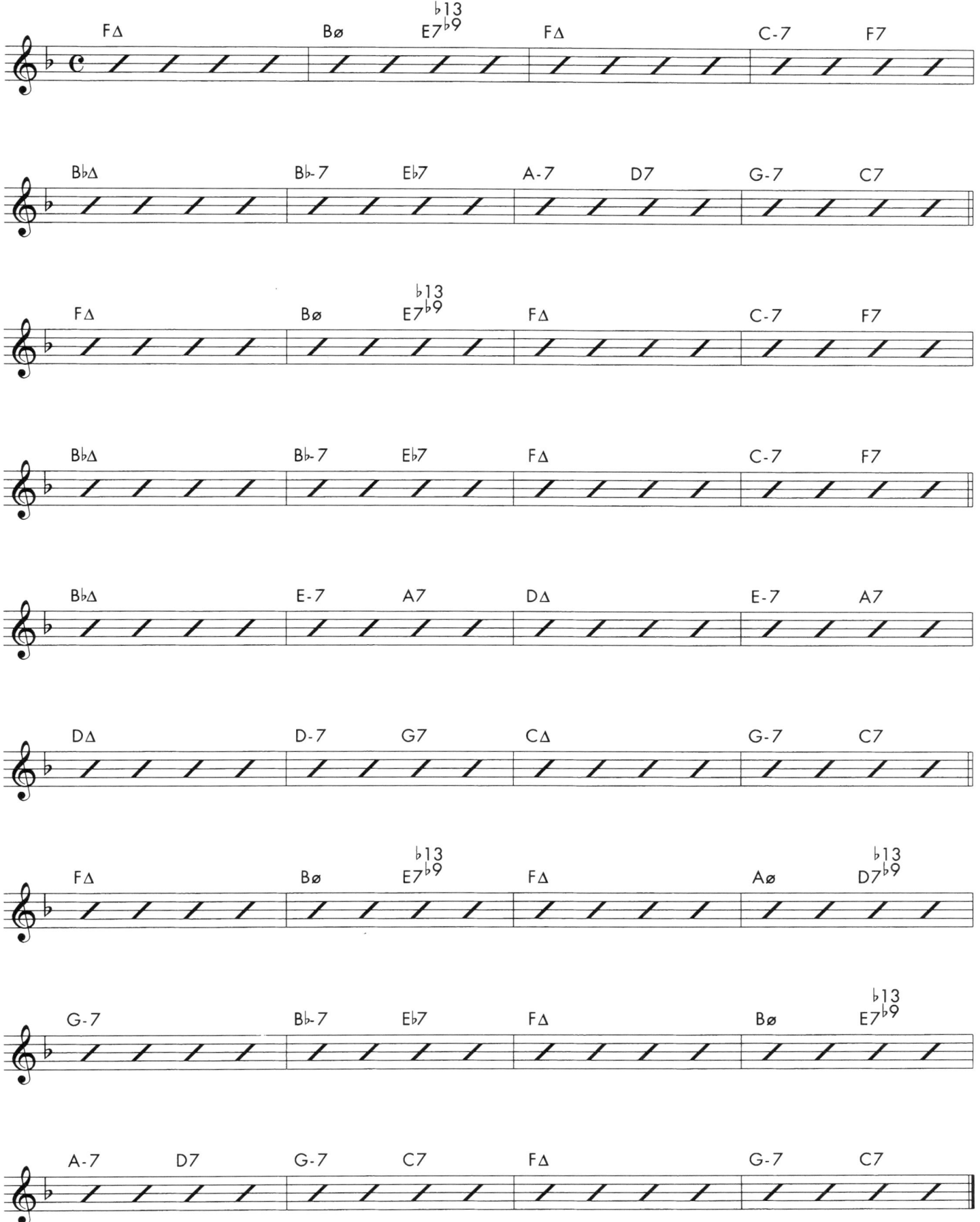

VIII PRACTICE EXERCISES

TUNE #8 "YOU'RE THE ONE"

B♭ Instruments

VIII PRACTICE EXERCISES

TUNE #8 "YOU'RE THE ONE"

Eb Instruments

IX FOUR NOTE GROUPINGS 5-9

As you might have guessed the next grouping of numbers to consider are the 5 - 9's. Until now we have focussed our attention on the basic triad of the chord (1 - 5). We are now going to move into the intermediate part of the chord and expand our improvisational vocabulary by adding the melodic segments which are found between the fifth and ninth degrees of the chord.

5-9 GROUPINGS: 5-6-7-9, 5-7-8-9

For major and dominant chords the four note grouping is 5-6-7-9 and for minor chords it is 5-7-8-9. (Note that "9" is the same as "2" and "13" is the same as "6". See Chapter XI for explanation.)

In order to determine the notes which correspond to these numbers you might find it necessary to refer back to our discussion of chord scales in Chapter 1. You can also refer to the scale chart in the Appendix.

The 5 - 9 groupings for major and dominant chords are no longer the same as is the case with the 1 - 5 grouping. A major 7 chord uses the 7 of the major chord scale while the dominant 7 chord uses the flat 7 of the major scale; hence the numbers 5-6-7-9 reflect what is implicit in each scale. The 7 of C dominant 7 means flat 7 or "B♭" while the 7 of C major 7 means natural 7 or "B".

Note: In order to simplify matters, all numbers for each type of chord are being compared to the major, dominant or minor scales. The numbers will be preceded by a flat or sharp alteration only when the appropriate scale contains notes which differ from one of those three scales.

For example, a C minor 7♭5 chord scale is C-D♭-E♭-F-G♭-A♭-B♭-C, so it follows that the numbers will reflect the altered 5 and 9 while the 7 carries no accidental because it doesn't differ from a minor chord scale, ♭5-7-8-♭9 means G♭-B♭-C-D♭.

5-9 PERMUTATIONS

As with the 1 - 5 grouping, there are 24 permutations of 5-6-7-9 and 5-7-8-9. Notice that 8 of the minor scale will replace 7 of the major and dominant scales and 7 of the minor will replace 6 of the major.

5	6	7	9	Major and Dominant
5	7	8	9	Minor

24 Permutations of 5-6-7-9

5 6 7 9	6 9 5 7	7 6 5 9	9 5 6 7
5 6 9 7	6 9 7 5	7 6 9 5	9 5 7 6
5 7 6 9	6 7 5 9	7 9 5 6	9 7 6 5
5 7 9 6	6 7 9 5	7 9 6 5	9 7 5 6
5 9 6 7	6 5 7 9	7 5 6 9	9 6 5 7
5 9 7 6	6 5 9 7	7 5 9 6	9 6 7 5

24 Permutations of 5-7-8-9

5 7 8 9	7 9 5 8	8 7 5 9	9 5 7 8
5 7 9 8	7 9 8 5	8 7 9 5	9 5 8 7
5 8 7 9	7 8 5 9	8 9 5 7	9 8 7 5
5 8 9 7	7 8 9 5	8 9 7 5	9 8 5 7
5 9 7 8	7 5 8 9	8 5 7 9	9 7 5 8
5 9 8 7	7 5 9 8	8 5 9 7	9 7 8 5

The 5-6-7-9 melody for major chords is identical to the major grouping 1-2-3-5 displaced by a fifth. 5-6-7-9 of C major is the same as 1-2-3-5 of G major. Similarly, the minor grouping 5-7-8-9 is identical to the minor grouping 1-3-4-5 displaced by a fifth. 5-7-8-9 of C minor is the same as 1-3-4-5 of G minor.

5-6-7-9 of C major = 1-2-3-5 of G major

5-7-8-9 of C minor = 1-3-4-5 of G minor

The first step in practicing the 5 - 9 grouping is to select four permutations; one beginning with 5, one beginning with 6, one beginning with 7, and one beginning with 9, and play them through a tune. Remember to make the appropriate replacements for the minor chords. The following examples illustrate the use of permutations 5-6-7-9 and 7-9-6-5 on the first eight bars of Tune #2.

IX FOUR NOTE GROUPINGS 5-9

Example # 6 (C Treble Clef Instruments)
Grouping 5-6-7-9

Example # 6 (B♭ Instruments)
Grouping 5-6-7-9

Example # 6 (E♭ Instruments)
Grouping 5-6-7-9

Example # 6 (Bass Clef Instruments)
Grouping 5-6-7-9

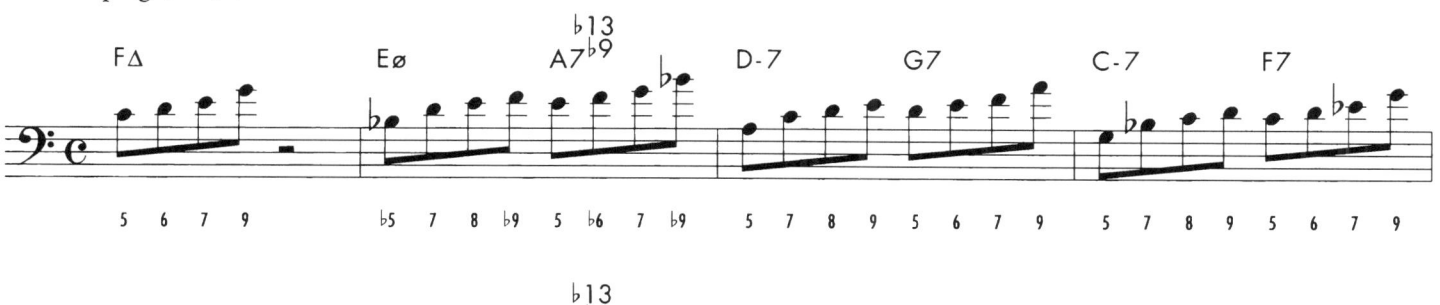

Example # 7 (C Treble Clef Instruments)
Grouping 7-9-6-5

Example # 7 (B♭ Instruments)
Grouping 7-9-6-5

IX FOUR NOTE GROUPINGS 5-9

Example # 7 (E♭ Instruments)
Grouping 7-9-6-5

Example # 7 (Bass Clef Instruments):
Grouping 7-9-6-5

ASSIGNMENT IX

This assignment is equivalent to the first eight chapters of this book. Because it is an extensive amount of work treat each step of the assignment as if it were a chapter.

1. On Tune #1 or Tune #2, play the following permutations:

For Major and Dominant	For Minor
a) 5 6 7 9	5 7 8 9
b) 6 5 9 7	7 5 9 8
c) 7 9 6 5	8 9 7 5
d) 9 7 6 5	9 8 7 5

   Remember visualizing these numbers as block chords will greatly facilitate your command of these numbers.

2. Mix up any 5 - 9 permutations randomly on the same tune seeking variety in your melodic lines.

3. Add the technique of editing to these solos.

4. Add the use of inversions to these solos.

5. Do the chord progressions in Chapter VIII using the 5 - 9 groupings.

6. As with the 1 - 5 grouping, review skills of the 5 - 9's.

X AVOID NOTES

"4" OF MAJOR OR DOMINANT

The fourth degree of the major and dominant scales is the only scale tone not included in either the 1-2-3-5 or 5-6-7-9 groupings. This note is referred to as an "avoid note" although that is a misnomer. It is not really a note which one should avoid but rather a note which requires special consideration.

Because of the half step interval between the third and the fourth notes of the major or dominant scale, "landing" on the four sounds dischordant. That is, over emphasizing the four sounds dissonant as a result of the flat nine interval between three and four. The four therefore needs to be resolved in some way. For example, it can be resolved down to the third or up to the fifth. The following melodies demonstrate how this can be accomplished:

"6" OF MINOR

Similarly, the sixth degree of the minor scale is the only scale tone not included in either the 1-3-4-5 or 5-7-8-9 groupings. The six also requires special consideration as it is a pungent sounding note. Because the six is a half step from the seven and a tritone away from the flat three, it creates some dissonant intervals as well. It also suggests a dominant sound because of the tritone interval between the flat three and the sixth.

The six doesn't require resolution in the same way as the four of the major scale but it is important to recognize its distinct sound. Like the sharp eleven sound on a major chord, the six on a minor chord jumps out at you.

Note that the six is often used on a tonic minor. (Tonic minor is the one chord in a minor key.) For example, in the key of C minor it is common to use the sixth degree, "A", when voicing the tonic chord.

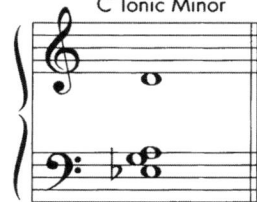

ASSIGNMENT X

1. Play through Tune #9 resolving the four to three on every chord change. For the purpose of keeping the exercise consistent, resolve the four on minor chords even though in the case of minors it is not necessary.

   Example:

   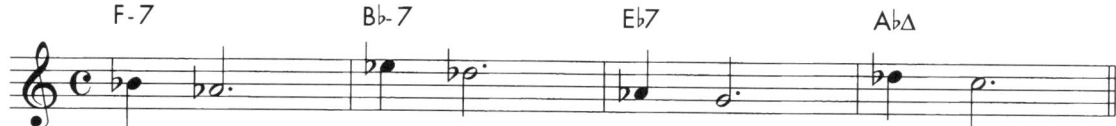

2. Play through these same changes resolving the four up to five.

   Example:

   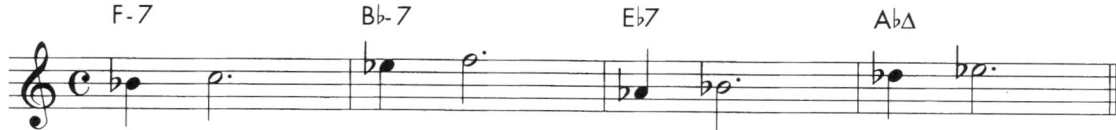

3. Repeat the exercise using the melody 4-#4-6-5 as an embellished resolution of four.

   Example:

4. On Tune #9, begin a melody with four on each chord change and vary the ways of "leaving" it. Try using resolutions which have not been mentioned.

X AVOID NOTES

TUNE #9 "FANGS FROM AFAR"

Concert Instruments

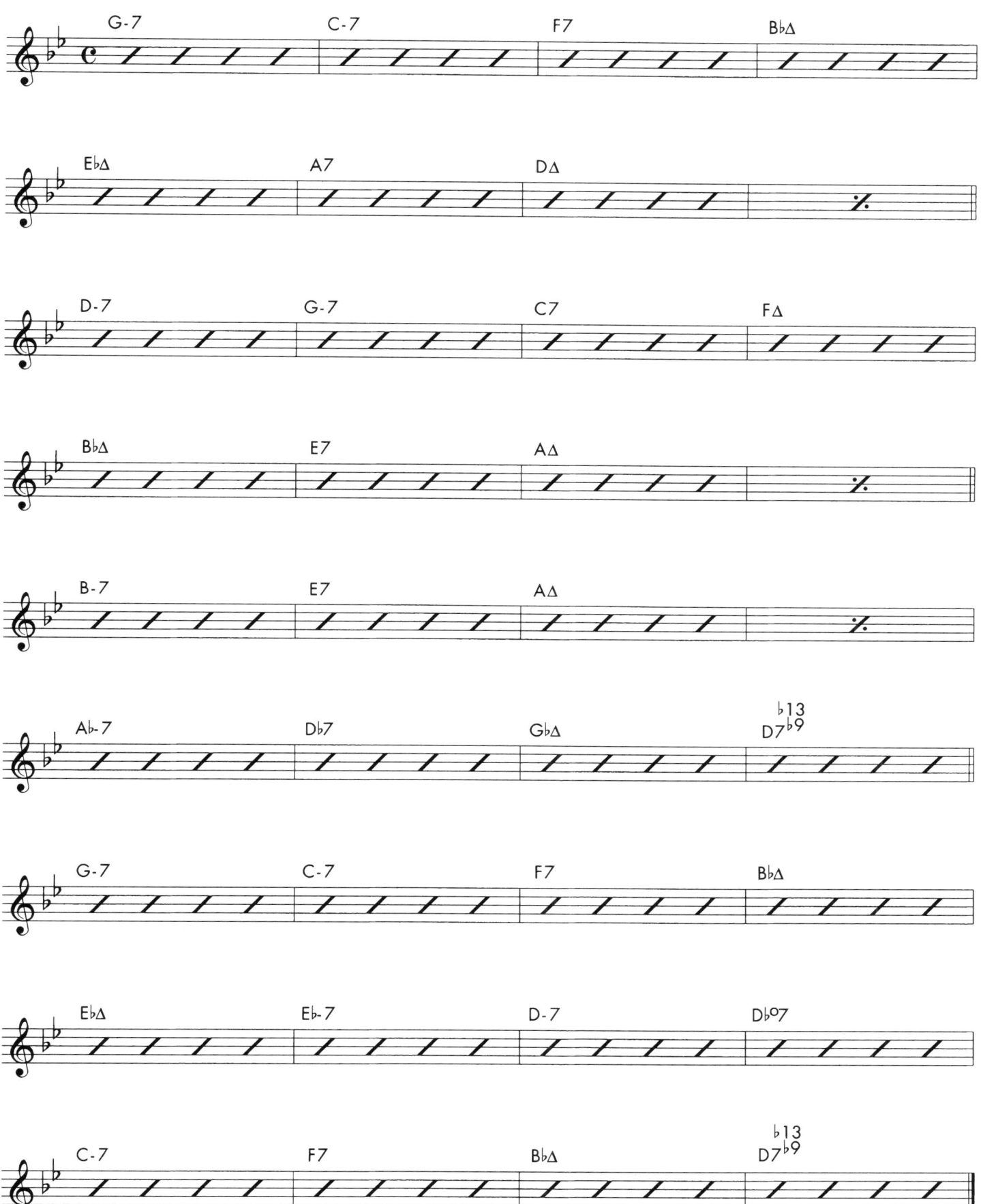

X AVOID NOTES

TUNE #9 "FANGS FROM AFAR"

E♭ Instruments

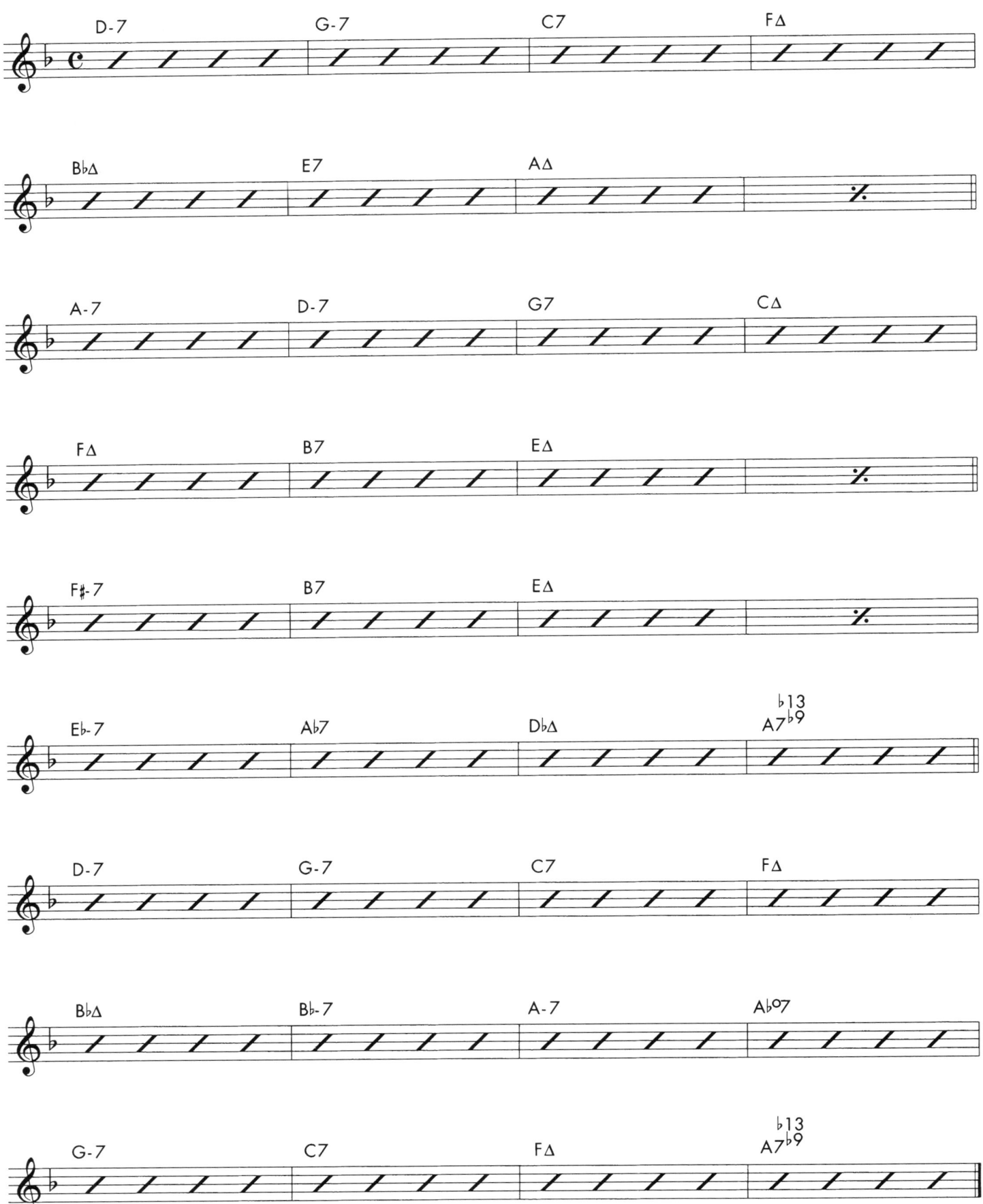

XI UPPER STRUCTURE GROUPINGS 9-13

TENSIONS

The music of today incorporates not only triads and seventh chords but ninths, elevenths, and thirteenths as well. Theses notes 9, 11, and 13, are upper chord tones and are called "upper structure" notes or "tensions". They are particular chord tones which add different sounds to the basic tonality of the chord; that is, 9, 11, and 13, are extensions of 1, 3, 5, and 7. Think of every chord as if it were a rainbow, the 1-3-5-7 being the primary colors and the 9-11-13 the secondary colors.

Tensions derive their numbers from the second octave of the chord scale.

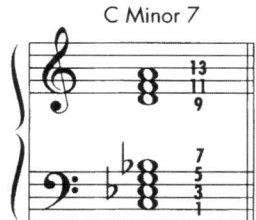

9 is the same as 2

11 is the same as 4

13 is the same as 6

♭9 is the same as ♭2

♯11 is the same as ♯4

Each type of chord uses specific colors or tensions:

Major chords use: 9, ♯11, and 13

Minor chords use: 9, 11, and 13

Dominant chords use: 9, ♭9 or ♯9, ♯11, 13 or ♭13

Notice that the dominant chord is more versatile in that it can use a greater variety of tensions. ♯11 is used on dominant and major chords because it doesn't need to be resolved, whereas the natural 4 does. As discussed in the previous chapter, the reason the natural four wants to be resolved is because of the half step interval between the third and fourth notes of the scale. The ♯11 sounds less dissonant as it creates a natural 9th interval to the third.

GROUPINGS 9-13: 9-10-#11-13, 9-11-12-13

The next four note grouping to consider incorporates tensions or upper structure notes; that grouping is 9-10-#11-13 for major and dominant chords and 9-11-12-13 for minor chords. As with the previous groupings 1 - 5 and 5 - 9, make the appropriate flat or sharp alterations for minor 7♭5 chords and dominant 7♭9♭13 chords according to their respective scales.

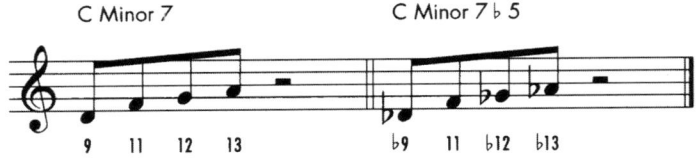

These upper structure notes take some getting used to. At first they might sound peculiar to you but with practice they will become more familiar. "Ear training" is always a beneficial side effect when practicing any set of numbers or grouping of notes. If you play 9-10-#11-13 often enough you will know that sound and be able to recognize it. One of the things which differentiates one player from another is each individual's use of different colors. The modern musician recognizes the unique sound of each chord tone and puts them to use in his or her improvisation.

9-13 PERMUTATIONS

As with the other groupings of notes, there are 24 permutations of 9-10-#11-13 for major and dominant chords.

24 permutations of 9-10-#11-13

9	10	#11	13	10	9	#11	13	#11	9	10	13	13	#11	9	10
9	10	13	#11	10	9	13	#11	#11	9	13	10	13	#11	10	9
9	#11	10	13	10	#11	13	9	#11	10	9	13	13	9	#11	10
9	#11	13	10	10	#11	9	13	#11	10	13	9	13	9	10	#11
9	13	#11	10	10	13	#11	9	#11	13	9	10	13	10	9	#11
9	13	10	#11	10	13	9	#11	#11	13	10	9	13	10	#11	9

Remember that when applying these numbers to minor chords, 12 of the minor replaces #11 of the major and 11 of the minor replaces 10 of the major.

9	10	#11	13	Major and Dominant
9	11	12	13	Minor

XI UPPER STRUCTURE GROUPINGS 9-13

24 Permutations of 9-11-12-13

9 11 12 13	11 9 12 13	12 9 11 13	13 12 9 11
9 11 13 12	11 9 13 12	12 9 13 11	13 12 11 9
9 12 11 13	11 12 13 9	12 11 9 13	13 9 12 11
9 12 13 11	11 12 9 13	12 11 13 9	13 9 11 12
9 13 12 11	11 13 12 9	12 13 9 11	13 11 9 12
9 13 11 12	11 13 9 12	12 13 11 9	13 11 12 9

Just as the 1- 5 grouping and the 5 - 9 grouping are symmetrically identical, so is the 9 - 13, it is simply displaced by yet another fifth.

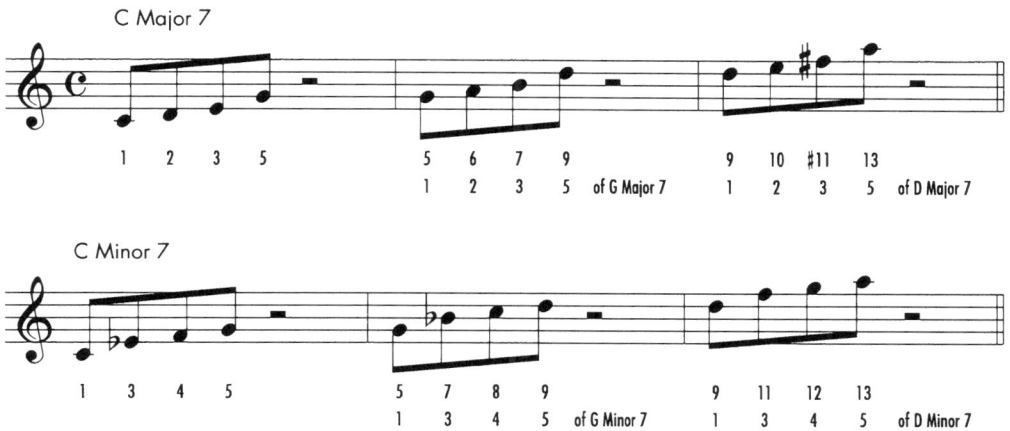

When studying these groupings of notes it becomes apparent how different chords begin to overlap. Note in the above example how 5-6-7-9 of C major is the same as 1-2-3-5 of G major and 9-10-#11-13 of C major is the same as 1-2-3-5 of D major. Similarly, 5-7-8-9 of C minor is the same as 1-3-4-5 of G minor and 9-11-12-13 of C minor is the same as 1-3-4-5 of D minor.

For The Advanced Player:

If we continue to build four note groupings upward in fifths, the melodies become polytonal with the use of 13-14-#15-17 and 17-18-#19-21 etc...

C major 7:   C - E - G - B - D - F# - A - C# - E - G# - B - D#

                  1 - 3 - 5 - 7 - 9 - #11 - 13 - #15 - 17 - #19 - 21 - #23

Perhaps a more practical way to envision these polytonal groupings is: 1-2-3-5 starting on six and 1-2-3-5 starting on three. For example, stacking groupings in fifths over C major would sound like this:

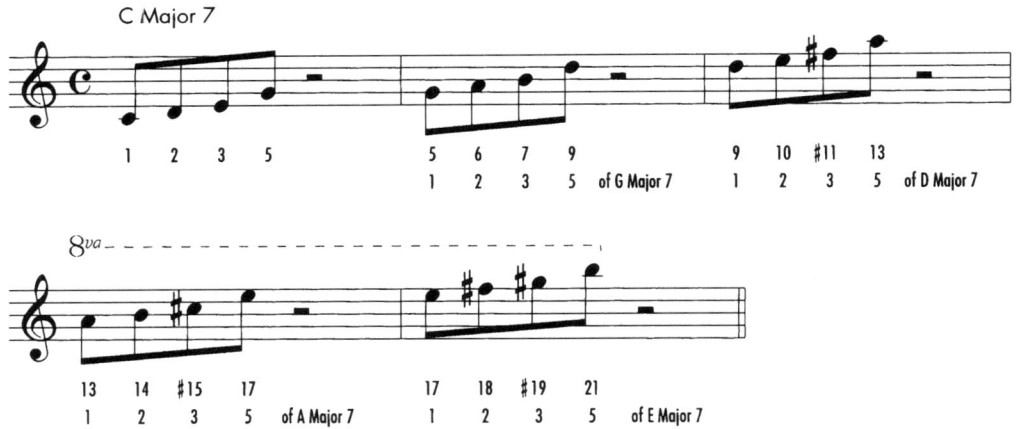

UPPER STRUCTURE TRIADS

Grouping or combining various primary or secondary chord tones allows us to form numerous triads within any given chord. These triads are called "upper structure triads". For example, on a C dominant 7 chord, the 9 #11, and 13 form a "D" triad. The following are some other examples of upper structure triads on a C dominant 7 chord:

When applying the number system, that is playing 1-2-3-5 or 1-3-4-5 of these upper structure triads, the relationships between different chords becomes even more intricate!

ASSIGNMENT XI

1. On Tune #1 or Tune #2 play the following permutations:

For Major and Dominant	For Minor
a) 9-10-♯11-13	9-11-12-13
b) 10-9-13-♯11	11-9-13-12
c) ♯11-13-10-9	12-13-11-9
d) 13-11-10-9	13-12-11-9

   The examples at the end of this assignment will help you to get started.

   In order to hear the distinct sound of each note against the basic chord tonality it is necessary to play the chord as well, otherwise the 9-10-♯11-13 will sound like 1-2-3-5 of another chord.

2. Mix up any 9 - 13 permutations randomly on the same tune seeking variety in your melodic lines.

3. Add the technique of editing to these solos.

4. Add the use of inversions to these solos.

5. Do the exercise in Chapter VIII using the 9 -13 groupings.

6. As with the previous groupings, review your skills using the 9 - 13's.

Assignment 1a:

Assignment 1c:

XII ADDITIONAL GROUPINGS

In the previous chapters, three principal four note groupings of melodic scale segments have been discussed; 1 - 5, 5 - 9, and 9 - 13. These groupings overlap and form thirteenth arpeggios as they include all of the available chord tones for each chord.

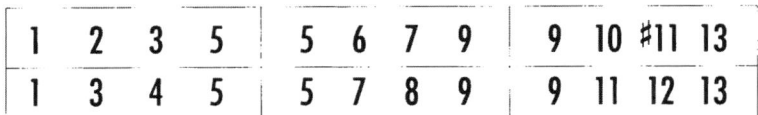

C Major 7

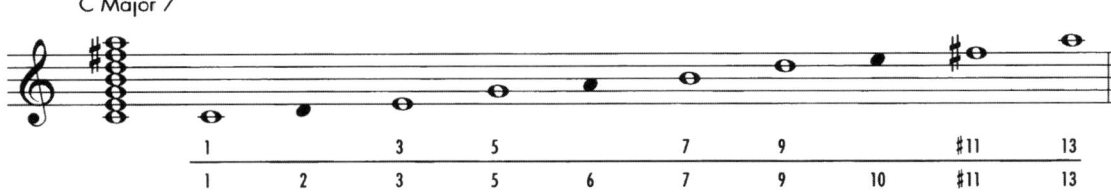

C Minor 7

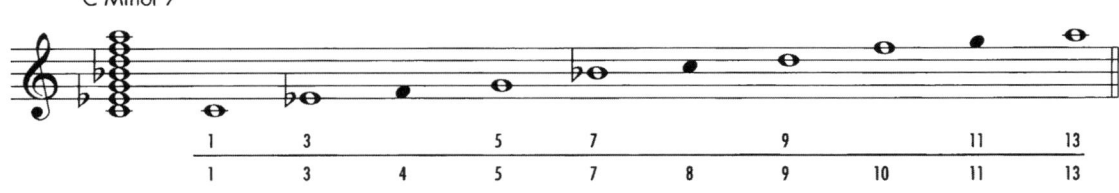

C Dominant 7

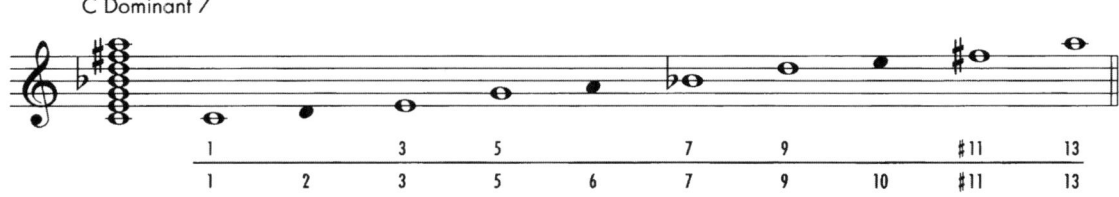

C Minor 7 ♭5

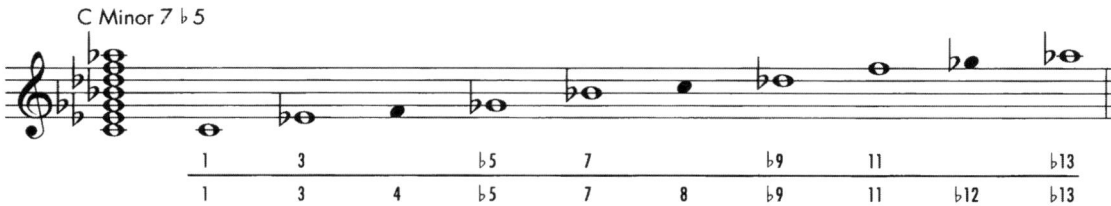

C Dominant 7 ♭9 ♭13

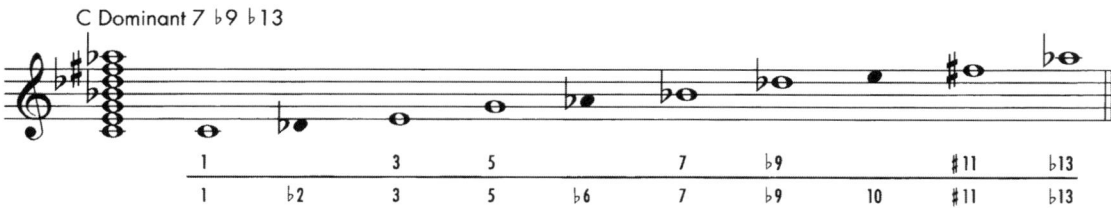

XII ADDITIONAL GROUPINGS

In addition to these scale segments, there are other groupings of notes worthy of attention as they add melodic material to our musical reservoir.

For Example:

$$3\ 5\ 6\ 7$$

$$3\ 4\ 5\ 7$$

$$7\ 9\ 10\ \sharp 11$$

$$7\ 8\ 9\ 11$$

$$\sharp 4\ 6\ 7\ 8 = \sharp 11\ 13\ 14\ 15$$

$$4\ 5\ 6\ 8 = 11\ 12\ 13\ 15$$

$$6\ 7\ 8\ 10 = 13\ 14\ 15\ 17$$

$$6\ 8\ 9\ 10 = 13\ 15\ 16\ 17$$

3-7 GROUPINGS

The four note grouping 3-5-6-7 is a significant melodic segment as it includes both the third and seventh of the chord. These notes are called "guide tones" and they are the most important notes in describing the quality of the chord, that is, whether the chord is major, dominant, or minor, is determined by the third and the seventh. They are the notes which actually give the chord its particular sound.

The grouping 3-5-6-7 is used on major and dominant chords and 3-4-5-7 is used on minor chords; the 4 of the minor replaces the 5 of the major and the 5 of the minor replaces the 6 of the major.

| 3 | 5 | 6 | 7 | Major and Dominant |
| 3 | 4 | 5 | 7 | Minor |

Notice how 3-5-6-7 of C major is the same as 1-3-4-5 of E minor and 5-7-8-9 of A minor, or how 3-5-6-7 of C dominant 7 is the same as 1-3-4-5 of E minor $7^{\flat}5$.

XII ADDITIONAL GROUPINGS

The grouping 3-4-5-7 of C minor is the same as 1-2-3-5 of E♭ major, 5-6-7-9 of A♭ major, and 9-10-♯11-13 of D♭ major.

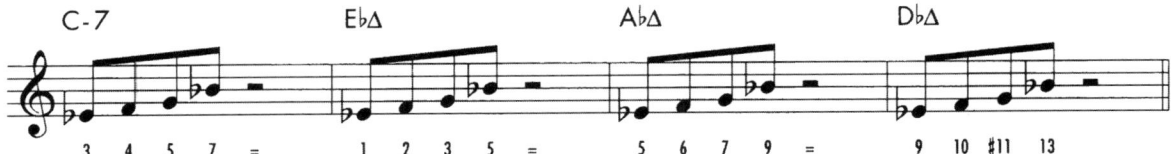

The grouping 3-4-♭5-7 of C minor 7♭5 is the same as 5-6-7-9 of A♭ dominant 7.

The point being made here is that the vast infinite chord universe gets more finite when you are able to see the similarities and common tones among chords. This becomes even more apparent when examining the upcoming scale segments.

7-11 GROUPINGS

The next grouping of notes to consider is the 7 - 11's. For major and dominant chords the numbers are 7-9-10-♯11, and for minor chords they are 7-8-9-11. 8 of the minor replaces 9 of the major and 9 of the minor replaces 10 of the major.

7	9	10	♯11	Major and Dominant
7	8	9	11	Minor

The similarities to other chords are listed in each column. For a minor 7♭5 chord you have the option of using either ♭9 or natural 9.

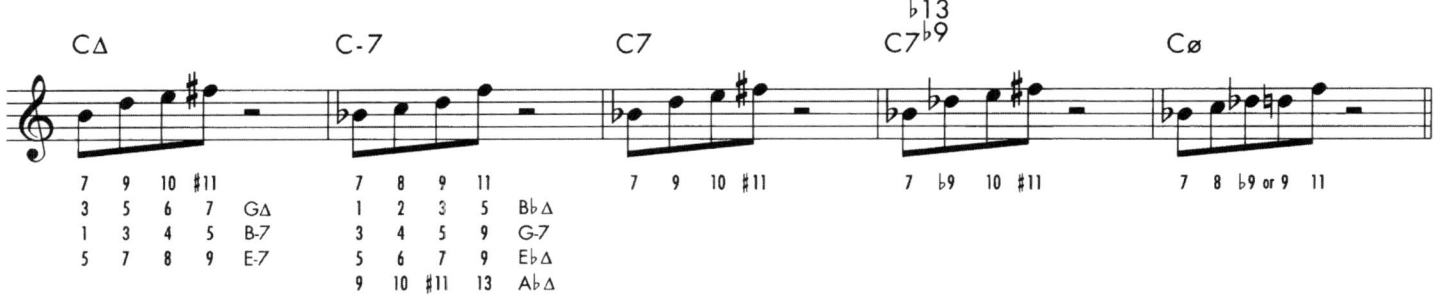

76

XII ADDITIONAL GROUPINGS

4-8 GROUPINGS

Another four note grouping includes the numbers #11-13-14-15 for major and dominant chords and 11-12-13-15 for minor. Perhaps it is more practical to think of this grouping in terms of the numbers #4-6-7-8 and 4-5-6-8, as 11 is the same as 4, 12 is the same as 5, etc...

#11	13	14	15	=	#4	6	7	8	Major and Dominant
11	12	13	15	=	4	5	6	8	Minor

6-3 GROUPINGS

Consider the grouping 6-7-1-3 for major and dominant chords and 6-1-2-3 for minor.

6	7	1	3	Major and Dominant
6	1	2	3	Minor

Creating these different four note groupings is one small way to organize melodic material. Each grouping has its own 24 permutations just as the 1 - 5's, 5 - 9's, and 9 - 13's. Other combinations of notes, such as 1-2-3-5 for minor or 1-3-4-5 for major, can also be used.

MELODIC SEGMENTS CAN FIT MANY CHORDS

A particular grouping of notes can fit many different chords. Becoming familiar with each type of chord and its appropriate chord scale enables you to envision a four note grouping as a segment of many scales. Take the four notes C-D-E-G, for example, and notice how many different chords this melody can be played over:

77

XII ADDITIONAL GROUPINGS

C Major 7	1-2-3-5
A Minor 7	3-4-5-7
D Minor 7 or D7sus4	7-8-9-11
F Major 7	5-6-7-9
G Minor 7 or G7sus4	4-5-6-1
B♭ Major 7 or B♭ Dominant 7	9-10-#11-13
E♭ Major 7	13-14-#15-17
E Minor 7♭5 or E Minor 7 (III-7 Key of C)	♭6-7-1-3
B Minor 7♭5	♭9-10-11-♭13
A♭ Major 7+5	3-#4-#5-7
F# Minor 7 or F#7 Alt	♭5-♭6-7-♭9
E Dom 7 Alt*	♭13-7-1-#9

* A Dominant 7 Altered chord scale is: 1-♭9-#9-3-♭5-♭13-♭7

Example: E7 Alt

Some of the above combinations used on certain chords have not been discussed previously and perhaps require some thought.

The following chart illustrates the numerous chords on which the melody C-E♭-F-G might be played over:

C Minor 7	1-3-4-5
A♭ Major 7	3-5-6-7
F Minor 7	5-7-8-9
D♭ Major 7	7-9-10-#11
B♭ Minor 7	9-11-12-13
A Minor 7♭5	3-♭5-♭6-7
G Minor 7♭5	4-♭6-7-1
G Minor 7 (III-7 in key of E♭)	11-♭13-14-15
E♭ Major 7 or E♭ Dominant 7	6-1-2-3
D Minor 7♭5 or D7sus4♭9	7-♭9-10-11
B Dominant 7 Alt	♭9-10-#11-♭13
A Dominant 7 Alt	#9-#11-♭13-14

XII ADDITIONAL GROUPINGS

ALTERNATIVE INTERVALLIC GROUPINGS OF 1-5

Up until this point we have considered a consonant approach to playing groupings of notes within the interval of a fifth. The following segments are some alternative intervallic groupings for 1 - 5. The term "intervallic" refers to the relationships between intervals within a melodic structure.

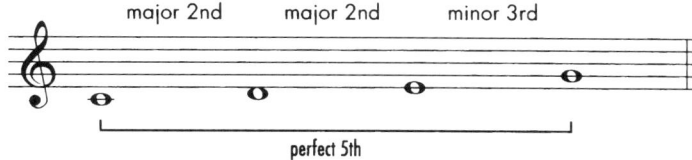

Some of the alternative structures listed below can fit conveniently on certain chords while others require further consideration. For example, the four note grouping C-F-F♯-G can be used on a C Minor chord scale. In this instance the F♯ acts as a "passing tone" to the fifth, it sounds right because it is resolved to the "G".

Ultimately, there are unlimited possibilities of four note groupings within this intervallic numerical system.

ASSIGNMENT XII

1. Take any additional grouping that you would like to work on; apply the same assignments as with the other groupings on the tune of your choice.

    a) Select four permutations.

    b) Mix them randomly.

    c) Edit your solos.

    d) Add the use of inversions.

    e) Repeat the exercises in Chapter VIII. Add a dominant cycle with ♭9 and ♭13.

    f) Review skills.

XIII MIXING GROUPINGS

Needless to say, the seasoned improvisor has all note groupings at his or her disposal. It isn't something that one is thinking about but rather information that one stores below the threshold of conscious thought. Just as riding a bicycle or reciting the alphabet are things we do without thinking, the improvisor is not thinking numbers while playing. Musicians derive their ideas from an inner reservoir of musical knowledge. The ability to freely improvise musical ideas is rooted in an understanding of harmonic and rhythmic concepts. It takes time and patience to "internalize" what has been consciously practiced.

The next step in this numerical system is to take the tunes which you've been working with and try to spontaneously use the many different groupings or tetrachords that have been discussed. Having all of these groupings at your disposal helps to facilitate good voice leading in your lines. For example, rather than play the following line on these chord changes,

you might play this instead:

This second example which employs mixing the 1 - 5 or 5 - 9 groupings yields a smoother line.

The following melody on the first eight bars of Tune #4 employs all of the four note groupings that have been discussed. Note that this example illustrates the various groupings and permutations before the technique of editing or the use of inversions is applied. Also, for the sake of visualizing particular groupings of notes, the enharmonic spelling of some chord tones has been used.

Example # 8 (C Treble Clef Instruments)

XIII MIXING GROUPINGS

Example # 8 (B♭ Instruments)

Example # 8 (E♭ Instruments)

Example # 8 (Bass Clef Instruments)

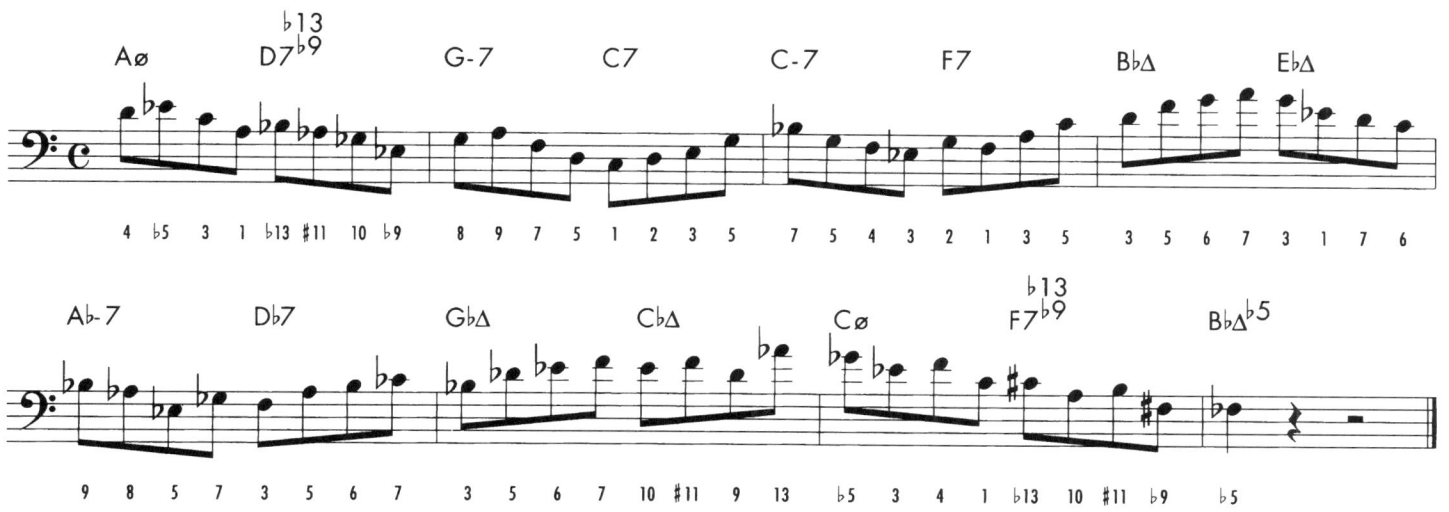

The following solos illustrate the use of all groupings and all concepts discussed in this volume.

XIII MIXING GROUPINGS

Example # 9 (C Treble Clef Instruments)

Example # 9 (B♭ Instruments)

Example # 9 (E♭ Instruments)

Example # 9 (Bass Clef Instruments)

XIII MIXING GROUPINGS

Example # 10 (C Treble Clef Instruments)

XIII MIXING GROUPINGS

Example # 10 (B♭ Instruments)

XIII MIXING GROUPINGS

Example # 10 (E♭ Instruments)

XIII MIXING GROUPINGS

Example # 10 (Bass Clef Instruments)

ASSIGNMENT XIII

1. Select one of the tunes which you have worked with and compose a melodic line through the chord changes using different groupings of numbers.

2. Repeat step one this time adding the technique of editing and the use of inversions to your composition.

3. Improvise step one on a tune of your choice.

4. Add step two to your improvisation.

CONCLUSION

Well, if you have gotten this far and you are able to use the number system described in this book, you've done quite a bit of work. Learning to play jazz is a building process like learning any new language and this system gives immediate results. It describes a method for acquiring a beginning vocabulary necessary for improvisation and for the more polished players it hopes to communicate some insights into that musical world. The information presented here is only a part of a much larger system. Other volumes in this series address different approaches.

We like to remind ourselves that becoming a great improvisor is a long range project. It never ends. It keeps expanding - that is the beauty of it.

I sincerely hope that the rewards have been worth your efforts.

APPENDIX

MAJOR 7 AND DOMINANT 7

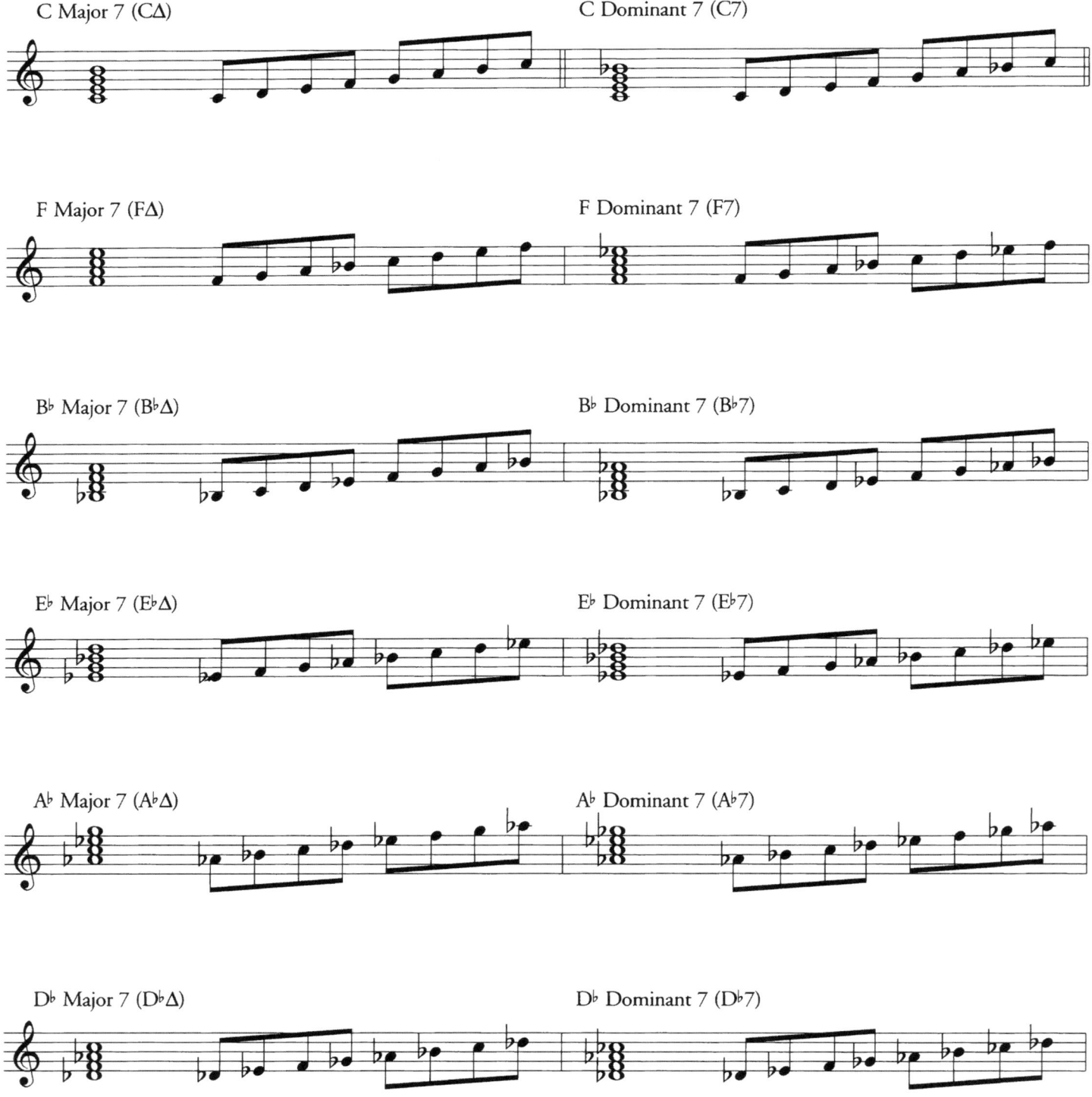

90

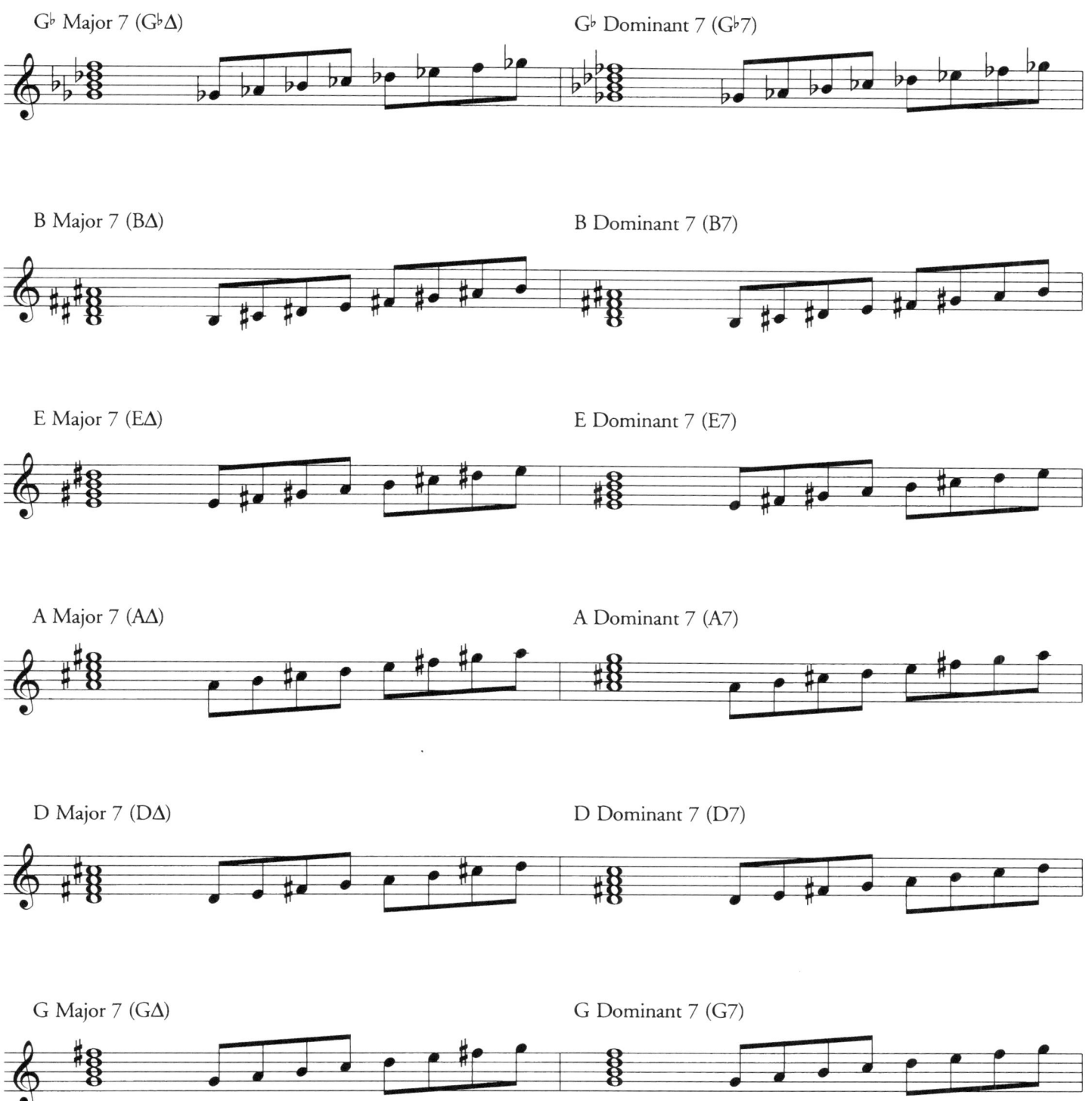

APPENDIX

MINOR 7 AND MINOR 7 FLAT 5

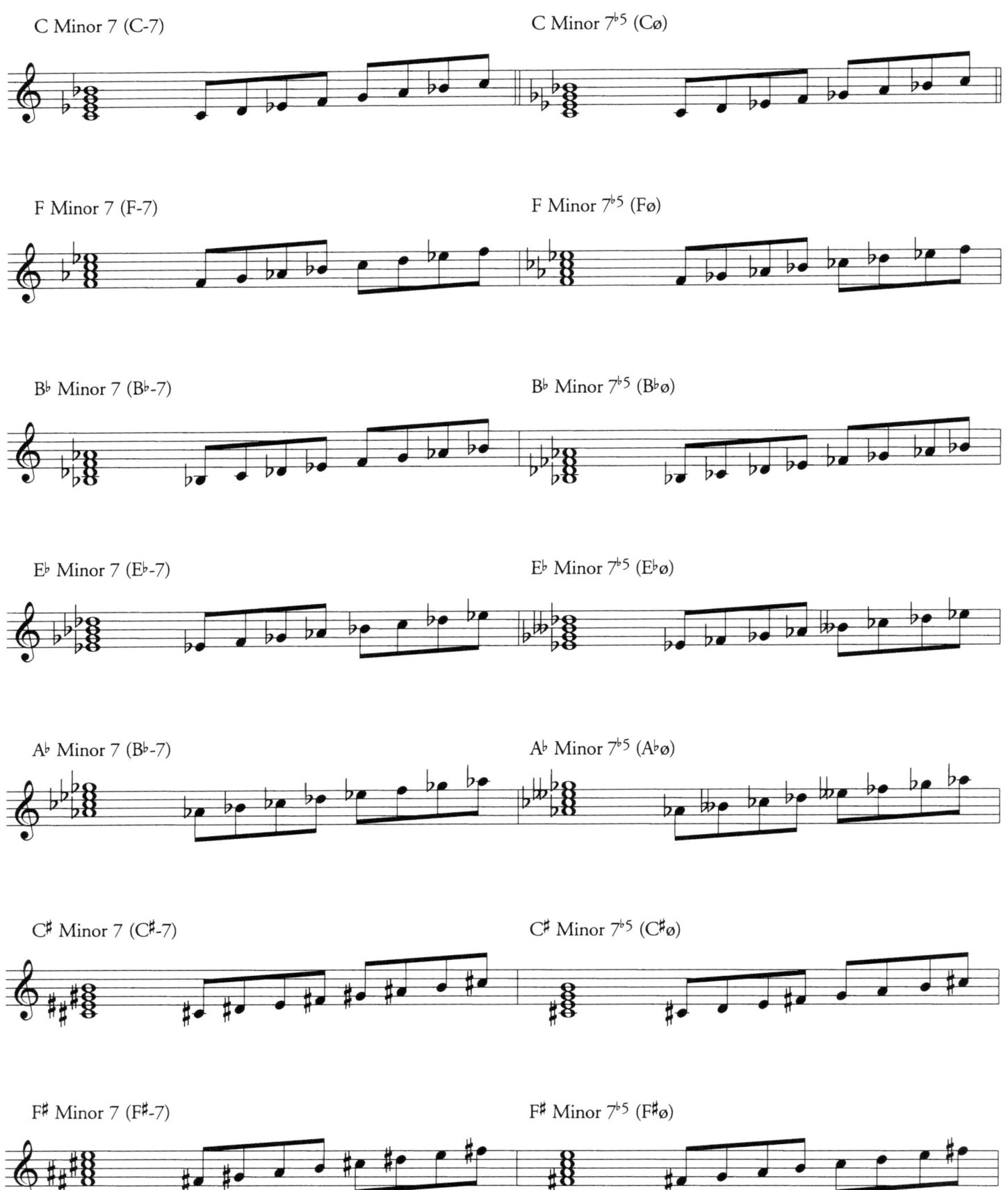

92

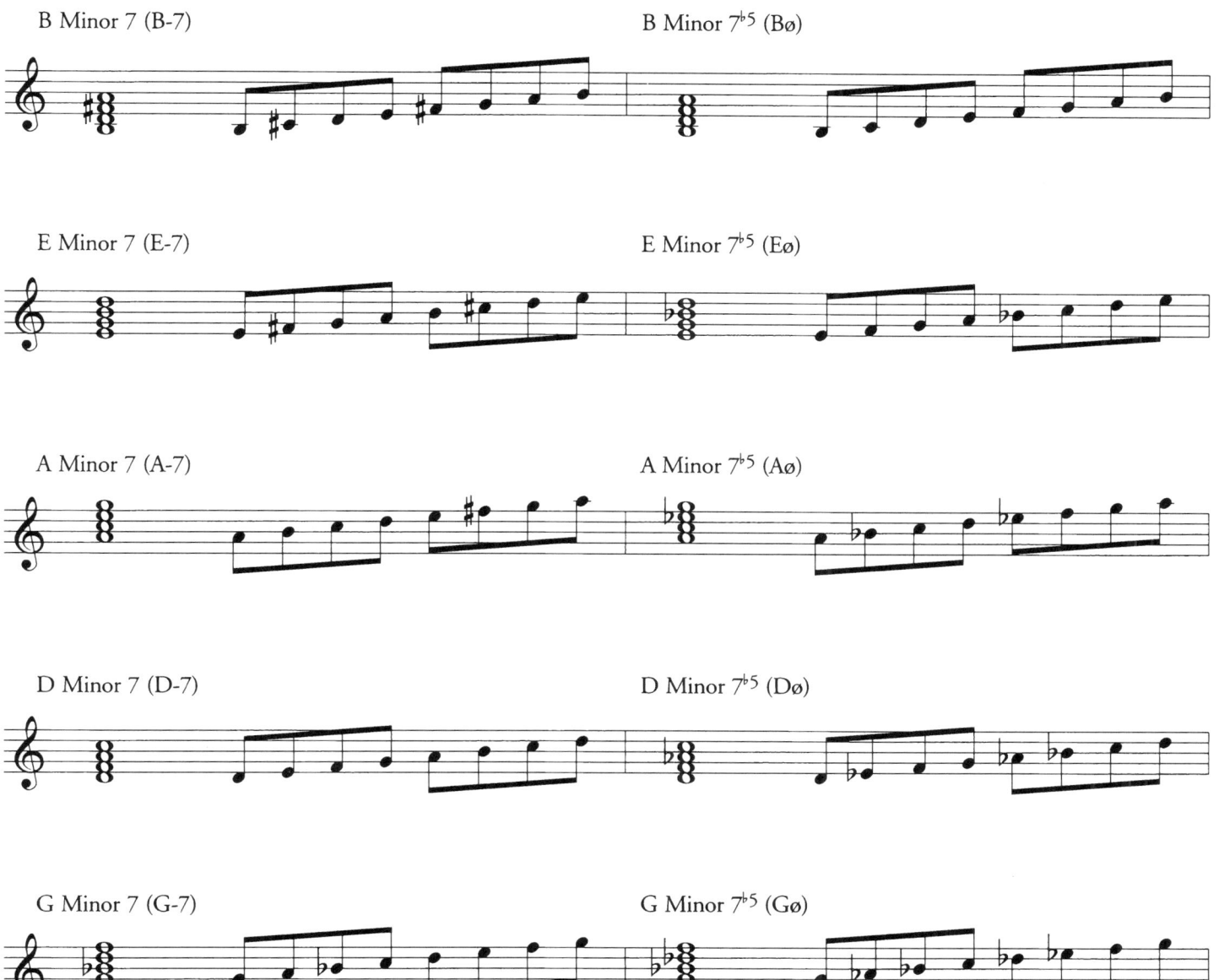

APPENDIX

DOMINANT 7 FLAT 9 FLAT 13 AND DOMINANT 7 ALTERED

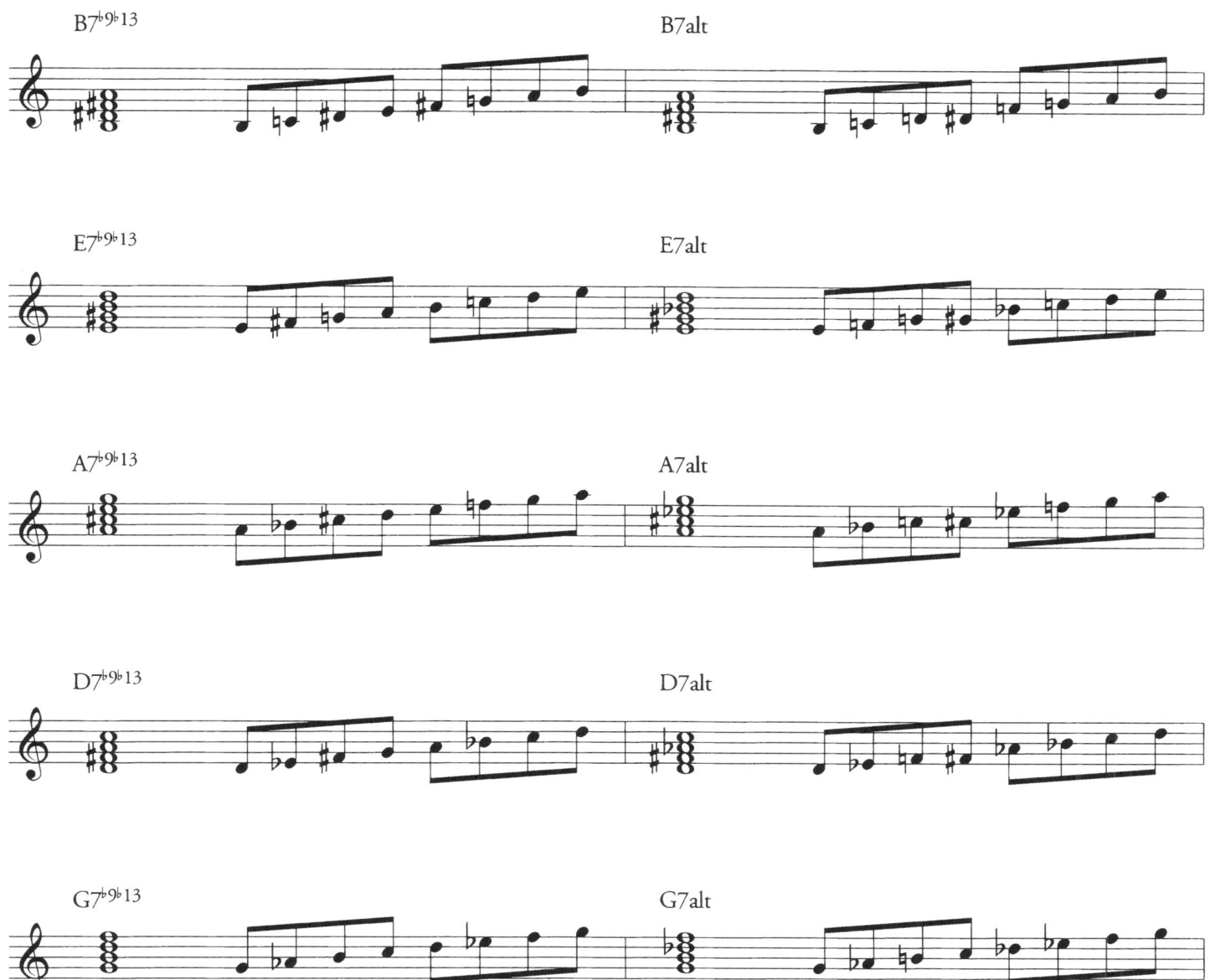

AUDIO TRACK LIST

 INSIDE IMPROVISATION, VOL. 1 »MELODIC STRUCTURES« – Jerry Bergonzi

PLAY-ALONG TRACKS	DEMONSTRATION TRACKS
1 Tuning Notes (Concert A and B♭)	**Assignment #1**
	20 Demonstration 1 on Tune #1
Tune #1	21 Demonstration 2a on Tune #2
2 Lady Duck (slow)	
3 Lady Duck (medium)	**Assignment #2**
	22 Demonstration 1 on Tune #2
Tune #2	
4 On the Brink (slow)	**Assignment #5**
5 On the Brink (medium)	23 Demonstration 2 on Tune #5
Tune #3	**Assignment #6**
6 Lunar (slow)	24 Demonstration 2 on Tune #6
7 Lunar (medium)	
	Assignment #7
Tune #4	25 Demonstration 1b on Tune #2
8 How Low the Sun (slow)	26 Demonstration 3 on Tune #2
9 How Low the Sun (medium)	
	Assignment #9
Tune #5	27 Demonstration 1a on Tune #2
10 Inside the Milky Way (slow)	28 Demonstration 3 on Tune #5
11 Inside the Milky Way (medium)	
	Assignment #10
Tune #6	29 Demonstration 4 on Tune #9
12 Brontosaurus Walk (slow)	
13 Brontosaurus Walk (medium)	**Chapter 13**
	30 Example 9
Tune #7	31 Example 10
14 Lovers Again (slow)	
15 Lovers Again (medium)	Jerry Bergonzi: Tenor Saxophone (tracks 20-31)
	Garry Dial: Piano
Tune #8	Dave Santoro: Bass
16 You're the One (slow)	Alan Dawson: Drums
17 You're the One (medium)	Recorded at The Outpost in Stoughton, MA.
	Engineer: Jim Siegel
Tune #9	Producer: Producer
18 Fangs of Afar (slow)	Executive Producer: Hans Gruber
19 Fangs of Afar (medium)	

© & ℗ 1994 Advance Music. All Rights Reserved.